FLOWERS

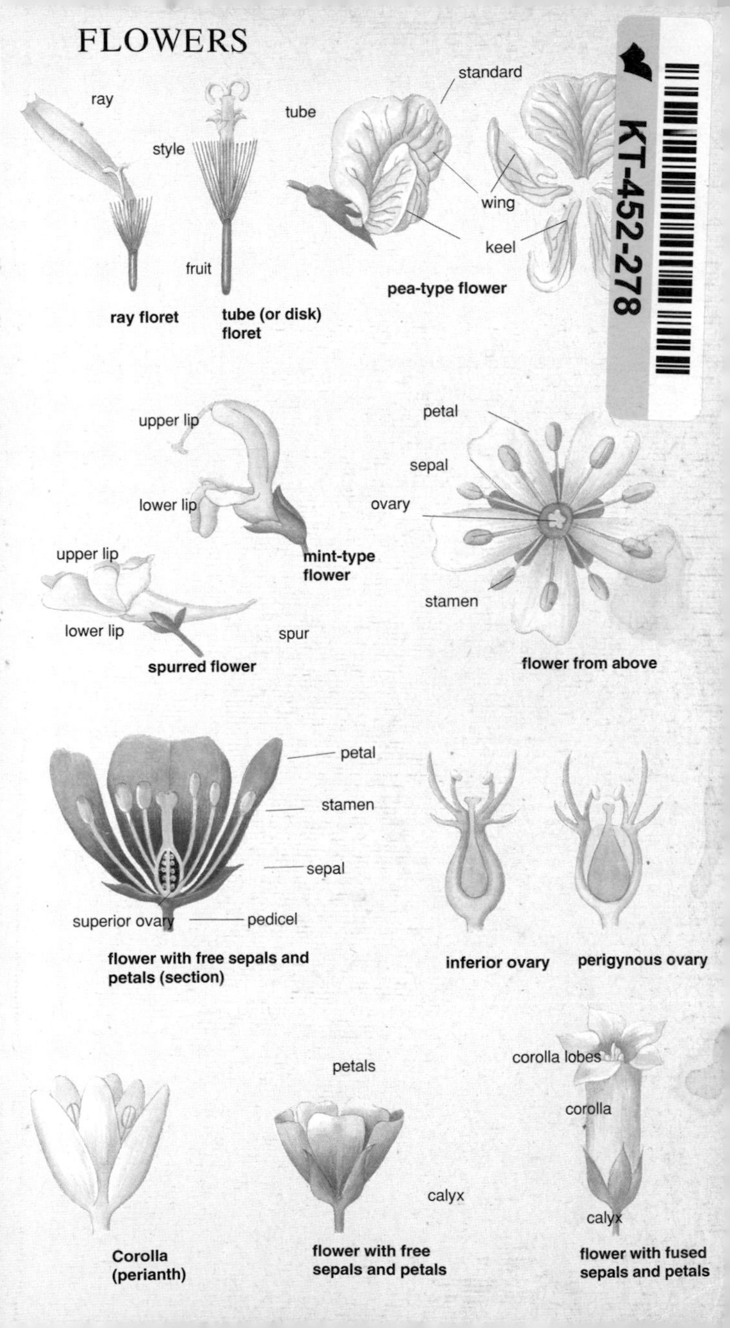

ray
style
fruit
tube
ray floret
tube (or disk) floret
standard
wing
keel
pea-type flower
upper lip
lower lip
mint-type flower
upper lip
lower lip
spur
spurred flower
petal
sepal
ovary
stamen
flower from above
petal
stamen
sepal
superior ovary
pedicel
flower with free sepals and petals (section)
inferior ovary
perigynous ovary
petals
calyx
corolla lobes
corolla
calyx
Corolla (perianth)
flower with free sepals and petals
flower with fused sepals and petals

Reprinted in 2008 for
Independent Book Sales

HarperCollins Publishers Ltd.
77-85 Fulham Palace Road
London W6 8JB

11 10 09 08
11 10

Written by Wolfgang Lippert and Dieter Podlech
Drawings by Heinz Bogner
This edition translated and adapted by Martin Walters

Translator's acknowledgement:
I should like to thank my father, Max Walters, for his advice and Anne James for her help with typing the translation.

Originally published in German as a GU Nature Guide
by Gräfe und Unzer GmbH, Munich

ISBN-13: 978 0 26 167403 5
ISBN-10: 0 26 167403 X

Collins uses papers that are natural, renewable and recyclable products made from wood grown in sustainable forests. The manufacturing processes conform to the environmental regulations of the country of origin.

Printed and bound in Singapore by Imago

FRUITS

DEHISCENT FRUITS

capsule (with teeth)

capsule (with pores)

capsule (with lid)

follicle

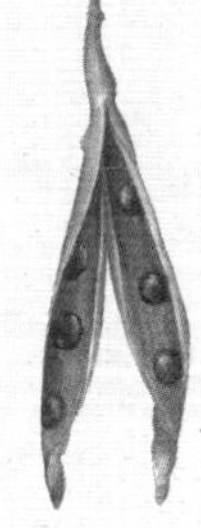

legume

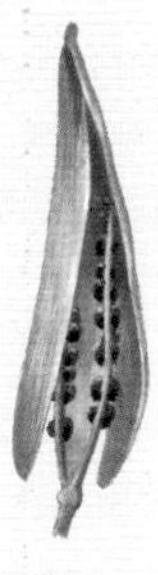

siliqua

INDEHISCENT FRUITS

nut

drupe

berry

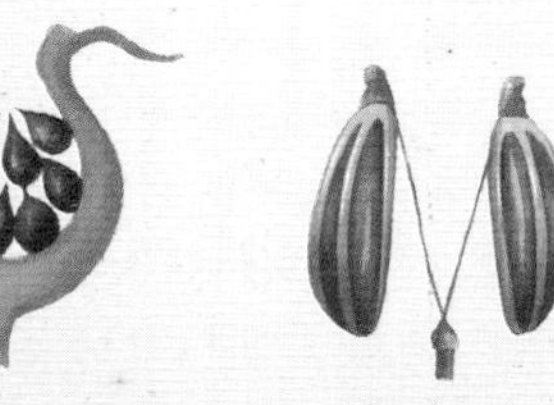

multiple or compound fruit

schizocarp

COLLINS
NATURE GUIDES

Collins · NATURE GUIDE

Translated and adapted by
MARTIN WALTERS

How to use this book

This plant guide is designed for identification in the field. The handy format, 400 colour photographs and over 100 informative botanical drawings make it ideal for taking on walks, nature rambles and similar trips.

The text and pictures include some of the best known flowering plants of the region. Not all the species included will be found wild in Britain and Ireland, but those which do grow there are clearly markedwith ✲. Some non-native mainland European species are nevertheless familiar as garden plants, and these are flagged [❀], as are native species which are also grown in gardens.

Colour-coded identification

The method used here for identification is straightforward. The species illustrated and described are arranged in groups according to flower colour. Coloured thumb markers at the edge of the pages simplify finding the flower colour sections. The first step in identification then is to choose the colour section. The second step involves identifying the plant using a combination of colour photographs and the botanical drawings. The latter are of important features such as flowers, fruits, leaves and growth form. Within each colour group the species are arranged in the same sequence, according to their place within the larger systematic groups (genus, family).

The five colour groups

Blue contains all species with light to dark blue, or violet-blue flowers	pages 6-31
Yellow contains all species with light yellow to orange flowers	pages 32-91
Red contains all species with pink to dark red, purple or reddish-violet flowers	pages 92-155
White contains all species with white or cream flowers	pages 156-209
Green contains all species with greenish or brownish flowers	pages 210-237

Exceptions to the rule

Most species can be successfully tracked down by their flower colour. Using this method, plants with coloured sepals (e.g. Water Avens p. 180), and some with bi-coloured petals (e.g. Large-flowered Hemp-nettle, p. 72) can also be identified. There are, however, three particular, and rather rare exceptions:

- Flowers which change colour during the flowering period (e.g. Lungwort, p. 18)
- Flowers which vary in colour – particularly red/blue (e.g. Field Scabious, p 146), pink/white (e.g. Soapwort, p. 104), and pale yellow/white (e.g. White Bryony, p.186).
- Species with two or more different colour forms (e.g. Common Comfrey, p. 200)

Further practical help is provided by the BOTANICAL DRAWINGS on the front- and end-papers and within the descriptions. These show important features, such as the shapes of flower, fruit, stem and leaf, which reinforce the photographs, and help distinguish similar species. The short BOTANICAL SECTION at the end of the book (p. 238) gives basic technical information and complements that presented in the main text. The SPECIES INDEX (p. 245) makes it easy to find particular flowers. The CENTIMETRE RULE inside the cover will help you make measurements in the field.
Species protected in all or part of their range are marked with the symbol ☒, and poisonous species with the symbol ☠. ❀ indicates that the flower is commonly grown in gardens, often well outside its natural range.

Conservation

You should not pick or uproot any wild flower. Many rare species are specifically protected, and even common wild flowers may not be uprooted without permission. It is best to take photographs, or make drawings of wild flowers, leaving the live plants in their natural habitats for others to enjoy as well.

The text

The characteristics of each species are described in detail. Flower colour is one of the most obvious, and shape and flower type are the most important taxonomic features. The structure of the fruit is also important, since this character tends not to be altered by environmental conditions. Leaf shape, however, is often subject to environmental variation, as is the height of the stem and the amount of branching.

A plant's *flowering season* is influenced by the weather and seasons, and therefore by the precise site where it grows, be this a lowland or mountain location, or in the North or South of the region. For this reason the figures given encompass a relatively long period. The information on habitat is often a useful pointer to identification, although most species can grow in a range of different habitats. The commonest habitats are given in order of importance. The notes under *distribution* give an idea of the European, and sometimes the world, range of each species. To make identification of similar species easier, their distinguishing features are not only explained in the text, but are also shown in botanical drawings.

1 Bluebell* *Hyacinthoides non-scripta*

(Lily Family)

Well-known British wild flower, carpeting woods in spring and early summer. Grows in large patches on the woodland floor. About 50cm tall. The leaves are narrow and the bright blue (rarely white or pink) hanging flowers are bell-shaped, clustered together in groups of 4-16.
Flowering season: Apr-Jun
Habitat: Woods, hedges, banks.
Distribution: Throughout British Isles, but more scattered in S Ireland. Also Holland, Belgium and NW France.
Similar species: Garden Bluebells are usually a related species, *H. hispanica*, or hybrids between the two.

2 Small Grape Hyacinth ❀ ☒ *Muscari botryoides*

(Lily Family)

Hairless plant to about 25cm tall. Leaves grass-like, to about 8mm wide, narrowing towards tip. Flower spike dense, about 3-6cm long. Flowers conical and hanging, perianth segments almost completely fused. Scentless. Dark blue with white border and outwardly pointing teeth. 6 stamens; 1 short style; superior ovary.
Flowering season: Apr-May
Habitat: Meadows, open deciduous woodland; chalk.
Distribution: Much of Europe, especially warmer countries; sometimes escapes from gardens.
Similar species: Grape Hyacinth°, *M. neglectum*, has narrower leaves and slightly larger flower heads. W France and E Anglia.

3 Siberian Iris ❀ ☒ *Iris sibirica*

(Iris Family)

Grows in thick clumps to a height of about 1m. Leaves grass-like, 2-5cm wide, shorter than stem. Stem round, with 1-3 flowers in the axils of the higher leaves. Flowers light or dark violet-blue. Outer petals curved downwards, unbearded, paler towards centre, with dark veins; inner petals upright, somewhat darker than outer petals. Fruit a capsule, to about 5cm long.
Flowering season: May-Jun
Habitat: Hay meadows, wet meadows, lake edges
Distribution: Europe (Germany, E France) – local, E to Japan.

FLOWER
Bluebell

1

Columbine* ❀ ☒

Aquilegia vulgaris

(Buttercup Family)

To about 60cm tall. Basal leaves long-stalked, twice trifoliate with toothed leaflets. Stem leaves smaller and unstalked. Flowers blue-violet, occasionally pink or white, sepals narrow and egg-shaped. Petals blunt with hooked spurs at base. Fruit has 5-8 elongated upright follicles.

Flowering season: Jun-Jul

Habitat: Woodland edges, wet woods, dry and damp grassland

Distribution: Central Europe. In Britain local N to S Scotland, and often a garden escape. Very local in Ireland.

2

Forking Larkspur* ❀

Consolida regalis

(Buttercup Family)

Annual to about 50cm tall. Leaves trifoliate, with narrow, linear, divided tips. Flowers clear blue, sepals oval, petals with long spur at the base. Fruit a single hairless follicle.

Flowering season: May-Aug

Habitat: Arable fields, farmland

Distribution: Europe, Turkey. Introduced and rare in Britain.

3

Monk's-hood* ☠ ❀ ☒

Aconitum napellus

(Buttercup Family)

Sturdy plant, to about 1.5m, usually with unbranched stem. Stem leaves deeply divided, with 3-7 lobes. Deep blue or mauve flowers in terminal cluster. Petals 5, uneven, the upper one curved over as a hood, and wider than long. Fruit 3 hairless follicles.

Flowering season: Jun-Aug

Habitat: High-altitude woodland, damp woods, river banks

Distribution: Europe, N to Britain and S Sweden, often in upland areas.

Similar species: *A. variegatum* has blue flowers, streaked with white, and hoods taller than broad. C. Europe.

A. septentrionale has long, tapering hoods. Scandinavia and NE Europe.

A. variegatum

FLOWER
Monk's-hood

4

Pasqueflower* ☠ ❀ ☒

Pulsatilla vulgaris

(Buttercup Family)

Hairy plant, to 30cm tall. Much divided basal leaves appearing after the flowers. Each stem has a single flower and a whorl of feathery leaves. Flowers violet, about 5cm long, at first bell-shaped, then opening out, shaggily hairy on the outside. Fruits to about 5cm long, with hairy achenes.

Flowering season: Mar-May

Habitat: Dry grassland on chalk

Distribution: C and W Europe, N to SE England (rare), Denmark and S Sweden.

1
2|3
4

1

Meadow Crane's-bill* ✿ *Geranium pratense*

(Crane's-bill Family)

Hairy plant to 1m tall, with forked stems. Basal and lower stem leaves with long stalks, and 5-7 deeply divided and toothed lobes. Stem leaves opposite, small. Flowers regular; 5 petals. Petals and sepals separate. Stems curve downwards after flowering, though sometimes curving upwards again eventually. Oval petals about 2cm long, violet or light blue, with darker veins. Stamens 10. Ovary superior, with long beak.
Fruit to 3cm long, with glandular hairs, ripening into 5 individual lobes, which remain connected at the beak, releasing the seeds as they bend upwards from the base.
Flowering season: Jun-Aug
Habitat: Damp meadows, stream sides, wet woodland
Distribution: From the Pyrenees to Japan, absent from parts of C Europe. In Britain commonest in Midlands and North.
Similar species: Wood Crane's-bill°, *G. sylvaticum*, has purple or pink-violet petals, and the stems remain upright after flowering. Not so common in lowland.
Hedgerow Crane's-bill°, *G. pyrenaicum*, has very hairy 5-9-lobed leaves, and purple-red flowers with deeply cut petals. S and C Europe, but introduced further N, including Britain and Ireland.

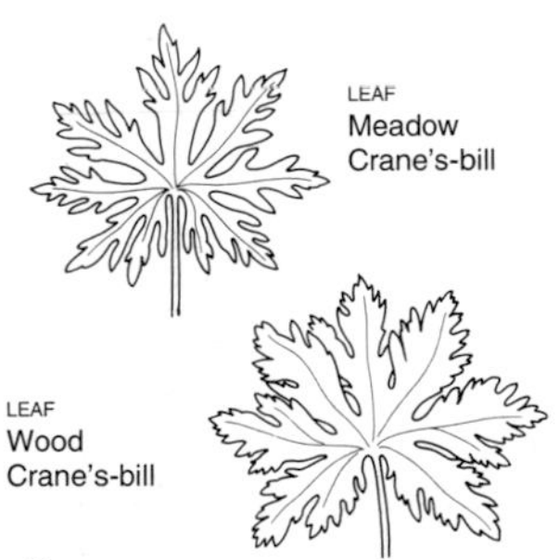

2

Hepatica ✿ *Hepatica nobilis*

(Buttercup Family)

To about 15cm tall. Many basal leaves, often overwintering, long-stemmed, glossy green above, brownish-red to violet below, and 3-lobed. Flowers single, on long hairy stalks. 3 sepal-like bracts beneath each flower. Flowers 2-3cm across, with 5-10 violet or pink (sometimes white) perianth segments (petals and petal-like sepals). Many stamens. Fruits hairy.
Flowering season: Mar-Apr
Habitat: Deciduous woods, scrub, on limestone
Distribution: Widespread, except on acid soils. Absent from British Isles and NW France.

1
2

1

Common Dog-violet*

Viola riviniana

(Violet Family)

Up to 20cm tall (very variable in size), this is one of the commonest violets. The flowers are scentless, about 25mm across and blue-violet, with purple lines in the centre. The spur is paler than the petals.
Flowering season: Mar-Jun
Habitat: Grassland and woods
Distribution: Common throughout region
Similar species: Early Dog-violet*, V. *reichenbachiana*, is similar but flowers 2-3 weeks earlier and has a dark spur. Most of Europe, as far N as S Sweden.

2

Marsh Violet*

Viola palustris

(Violet Family)

Low-growing, hairless species. Kidney-shaped leaves. Flowers scentless. Petals pale violet, the lowest one with darker veins. Spur straight and violet.
Flowering season: May-Jun
Habitat: Bogs, marshy woodland
Distribution: Most of Europe, getting rarer towards S and E.

3

Hairy Violet*

Viola hirta

(Violet Family)

Upright hairy plant to about 15cm tall. Leaves heart-shaped to triangular. Glandular hairs on leaf-stalks. Flowers scentless. Petals pale blue to violet, sometimes white. Spur dark and straight.
Flowering season: Apr-May
Habitat: Dry grassland
Distribution: Much of Europe, but only in S Scandinavia.
Note: There are about 25 species of violet in the region (including some with yellow petals). Those selected here are some of the commoner and more easily identified. The Sweet Violet, V. *odorata*, is widespread but often as a garden escape, and has many cultivated variants, some "doubled".

4

Common Milkwort*

Polygala vulgaris

(Milkwort Family)

A variable species, growing to about 30cm. The stems are rather feeble, with narrow, alternate leaves. The flowers (each up to about 8mm) superficially resemble those of the Pea Family. They may be blue, pink or white.
Flowering season: May-Sep
Habitat: Grassland, heaths and dunes
Distribution: Throughout most of region.
Similar species: Heath Milkwort*, *P. serpyllifolia* (plate 5), has slenderer stems with some opposite leaves and usually bright blue flowers. Throughout, but especially in N and W on acid moorland May-August. Dwarf Milkwort*, *P. amarella*, has unstalked basal leaves. Flowers small, blue, pink or white. Calcareous grassland. Only local in England.

1

2|3

4|5

1

Willow Gentian *Gentiana asclepiadea*

(Gentian Family)

To about 1m tall, with lanceolate, pointed stem leaves, each with 3-5 veins. Many flowers, 1-3 in leaf axils. Corolla to 5cm long, narrowly bell-shaped, blue, usually with violet spots inside, 5-lobed, with short teeth. Calyx with 5 short, narrow, pointed teeth.
Flowering season: Aug-Sep
Habitat: Fens, damp meadows, mountain woods, scrub; nearly always on limestone soils
Distribution: C and SE Europe, to Caucasus. Only in gardens in British Isles.

2

Marsh Gentian* ❀ ☒ *Gentiana pneumonanthe*

(Gentian Family)

To about 40cm tall, with narrowly lanceolate stem leaves, often rolled downwards at the edges, each with usually 1 vein. Fewer flowers than previous species, short-stemmed and in the axils of the upper leaves. Corolla to 5cm long, narrowly bell-shaped, blue with pale dots and a green midrib, 5-lobed with short teeth. Calyx with 5 narrow, pointed teeth.
Flowering season: Jun-Sep
Habitat: Fens, meadows, wet heaths
Distribution: Throughout, except far N, but nowhere common. Caucasus, Siberia. Very local in Britain and protected.

3

Spring Gentian* ❀ ☒ *Gentiana verna*

(Gentian Family)

To 15cm, with very short flower-stems. Basal leaves broadly lanceolate and pointed, up to 3cm long, much larger than the sparse stem leaves, and with small projections at the edges. Calyx winged along angles. Corolla deep blue, with a rather wide tube and spreading petal tips.
Flowering season: Mar-Aug
Habitat: Rocky and dry grassland, flushes; limestone
Distribution: Mountains of C and S Europe, Alps. Also Teesdale in Britain, and The Burren in W Ireland.

4

Fringed Gentian* ❀ *Gentianella ciliata*

(Gentian Family)

Hairless plant, to about 30cm, with upright, occasionally branched stems. Basal leaves spoon-shaped; stem leaves lanceolate and pointed. Flowers to 5cm long, blue. Corolla tube spreading about halfway along into 4 ovate lobes, each fringed with a beard of hairs. Calyx about half as long as corolla tube, with narrow sepals.
Flowering season: Aug-Sep
Habitat: Dry grassland, meadows, scrub, clearings; on limestone
Distribution: Much of C and S Europe; Caucasus, Turkey. Rare in Britain, on S chalk grassland.

1|2
3
4

1

Trumpet Gentian ⚘ ☒ *Gentiana clusii*

(Gentian Family)

Low-growing plant to about 10cm, with unbranched, very short stems. Lower leaves lanceolate and pointed, about 3-5cm, 3 to 5 times as long as wide. Stem leaves much smaller. Flowers solitary, corolla blue, 5-6cm long, bell-shaped, without green spots or stripes inside. Petals with triangular tips and small lobes between. Calyx teeth triangular, wider at base, 2.5-3 times as long as broad, roughly papillose at the margins. Deep divisions between calyx teeth. Stigma funnel-shaped, fringed.

Flowering season: May-Aug

Habitat: Scree, rocks, grassland, meadows, flushes; limestone

Distribution: Mainly in the limestone Alps; to lowland in Alpine valleys and foothills; Black Forest.

2

Autumn Gentian* *Gentianella amarella*

(Gentian Family)

Also known as Felwort, this is Britain's commonest gentian. Grows to about 25cm tall. The flowers have 5 lobes to corolla and calyx, and grow in dense clusters. They do not appear until late summer or autumn, and are usually dull purple (sometimes white).

Flowering season: Aug-Oct

Habitat: Chalk and limestone grassland, dunes

Distribution: Throughout, but rare in most of W Scotland and N Ireland.

Similar species: Field Gentian*, *G. campestris*. Flowers with 4 lobes; bluish-lilac (rarely white), July-October. Dunes and grassland. Throughout area. In Britain mainly in Scotland and Lake District; rare in Wales and most of England. In Ireland mainly in N and W.

1
2

1 Lesser Periwinkle* ❀ *Vinca minor*

(Periwinkle Family)

Hairless, to about 20cm tall. Non-flowering stems trailing, often rooting at nodes. Flowering stems upright. Leaves in opposite pairs, ovate, short-stalked and evergreen. Flowers solitary and stalked, growing from leaf axils. Corolla 2-3cm across, light blue, with short tube opening to a broad, flat face.
Flowering season: Apr-May
Habitat: Deciduous woods, scrub; calcareous soils
Distribution: Most of Europe, rarer towards the N; Caucasus, Turkey. Possibly native in S England; common in gardens.
Similar species: Greater Periwinkle*❀, *V. major*, has larger flowers and wider, slightly heart-shaped leaves.

2 Viper's Bugloss* ❀ *Echium vulgare*

(Borage Family)

A prickly-hairy plant growing to about 1m. Long lanceolate leaves, to about 35cm long at base of plant. Long, rather loose, cylindrical flowering spike, with many bright blue flowers (often reddish to begin with). Flowers with unequal petal lobes, and about 2cm long, hairy. Calyx split almost to base.
Flowering season: May-Oct
Habitat: Waste ground, open dry grassland, footpaths, quarries
Distribution: Most of Europe; also America.

3 Wood Forget-me-not* ❀ *Myosotis sylvatica*

(Borage Family)

Hairy plant to 40cm, with leafy stems. Leaves elliptical or lanceolate, with spreading hairs. Corolla blue, at 5-8mm across; opening out flat. Calyx after flowering to 5mm long, with hooked hairs.
Flowering season: May-Jul
Habitat: Meadows, open and damp deciduous woodland
Distribution: Widespread, except in N of region; often naturalized from gardens. S to Apennines and Balkans.
Similar species: Field Forget-me-not*, *M. arvensis* (plate 4), has very small bright blue flowers (to about 5mm across). Fields, woodland edge, roadsides, waste ground, dunes. *Flowering season:* Apr-Sep
Water Forget-me-not*, *M. scorpioides*, (calyx with flattened hairs), grows in wet habitats.

5 Common Lungwort* *Pulmonaria officinalis*

(Borage Family)

Hairy plant to about 30cm, with white-spotted leaves. Stem leaves clasping stem. The flowers start out pink, then turn gradually violet or blue.
Flowering season: Mar-May
Habitat: Shady places, particularly on heavy, clay soils
Distribution: C Europe, N to S Sweden and Holland. Introduced to Britain
Similar species: Narrow-leaved Lungwort*, *P. longifolia*, has more slender leaves, often unspotted. Rather western, N to France and S England.

1
2|3
4|5

1

Meadow Clary* ✿ ☒ *Salvia pratensis*

(Mint Family)

Softly hairy plant to about 1m. Square-stemmed. Basal leaves in a rosette, with a long stalk and irregular teeth. Stem leaves fewer and smaller, growing close to stem. Loose long spikes of whorled violet-blue flowers. Corolla to about 3cm, sickle-shaped and much longer than calyx.
Flowering season: May-Aug
Habitat: Dry grassland, hay meadows, grassy paths
Distribution: S and C Europe, N to N Germany and S England (rare in latter); Turkey, Caucasus, N Africa, N America.
Similar species: Wild Clary*, *S. verbenaca*, is smaller, with blue to violet flowers, and stickily hairy calyx. SE England and W France.

2

Skullcap* ✿ *Scutellaria galericulata*

(Mint Family)

To 60cm, with rectangular, somewhat hairy stem. Leaves short-stalked and ovate to lanceolate, basal leaves heart-shaped and toothed at edges. Flowers in pairs towards top of stem, in leaf axils. Corolla 1-1.7cm long, blue, lower lip with white spot. Calyx with short hairs, with a rounded, cap-like bulge on the upper side (hence name).
Flowering season: Jun-Sep
Habitat: Reed and sedge beds, wet meadows, river banks, swampy woodland
Distribution: Throughout region; Asia, N America.
Similar species: Lesser Skullcap*, *S. minor*, is smaller, has pink flowers and smaller, untoothed leaves. Usually in acid, wet soils.

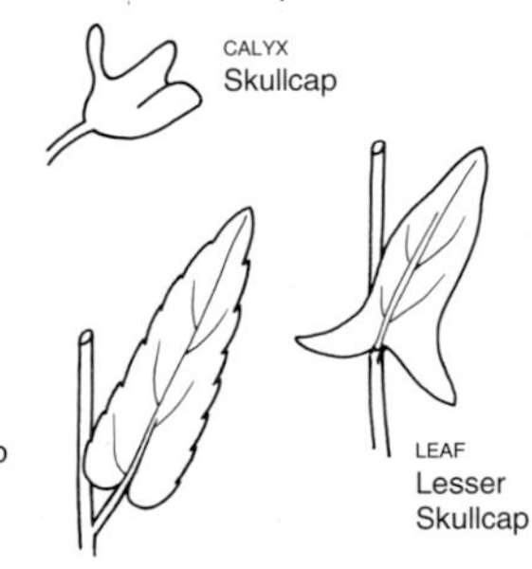

3

Selfheal* ✿ *Prunella vulgaris*

(Mint Family)

Sparsely hairy plant to 40cm with creeping stems. Leaves stalked and oval, basal leaves in rosette. Uppermost pair of leaves sits close to flower base. Flowers violet-blue, thickly clustered at tip of stem, and to 18mm long.
Flowering season: Jun-Sep
Habitat: Meadows, pastures, lawns, open woodland
Distribution: Europe, and spread worldwide.
Similar species: Large Selfheal, *P. grandiflora*, is larger, with flowers 2-3cm long, does not creep, and the uppermost leaf pair is well below flowers. Grassland. C Europe, as far N as S Sweden.

1|2
3

1

Ground-ivy* *Glechoma hederacea*

(Mint Family)

Creeping plant to about 20cm tall, rooting at the nodes, with erect flowering stems. Rounded blunt-toothed leaves, on long stalks. Flowers paired or in threes, in leaf axils. Corolla 1-2cm long; calyx with short hairs, to 7mm long.

Flowering season: Apr-Jul

Habitat: Deciduous woodland, scrub, woodland edges, meadows

Distribution: Most of Europe; Caucasus, Siberia.

2

Bugle* ❀ *Ajuga reptans*

(Mint Family)

Grows to about 30cm, with a basal rosette and long, leafy runners. Basal leaves stalked and almost spoon-shaped, stem leaves smaller and unstalked. Blue or violet-blue flowers in whorls in the axils of stem leaves. Corolla about 1-1.5cm long.

Flowering season: May-Sep

Habitat: Meadows, deciduous woods, scrub

Distribution: Most of Europe, as far N as S Norway; Caucasus, Turkey.

Similar species: Pyramidal Bugle*, A. *pyramidalis*, is found in C & N Europe. It has a very hairy stem, and purple flowers. It is a rare species in N Britain and Ireland.

3

Brooklime* *Veronica beccabunga*

(Figwort Family)

To about 60cm tall, hairless. Round stem, often rooting at nodes. Leaves short-stemmed and ovate, irregularly toothed. Flowers in opposite clusters in the axils of upper leaves. Corolla open and 4-lobed, 5-8mm across. 2 stamens. Fruit rounded capsules 3-4mm across.

Flowering season: May-Oct

Habitat: Stream sides, ditches, flushes

Distribution: Europe, N Asia, N Africa.

Similar species: Blue Water-speedwell*, V. *anagallis-aquatica*, has unstalked pointed leaves and pale blue flowers.

4

Germander Speedwell* *Veronica chamaedrys*

(Figwort Family)

To 40cm tall. Stem has two lines of hairs. Leaves ovate and toothed. Flowers in loose clusters in the axils of upper leaves. Corolla open, 4-lobed, to 15mm across; 2 stamens; calyx 4-lobed.

Flowering season: May-Aug

Habitat: Meadows, scrub, woodland edges

Distribution: Most of Europe, except far N; N and W Asia.

Similar species: Common (Heath) Speedwell*, *Veronica officinalis*, is smaller than Germander Speedwell, and with long-stalked flowering heads, with between 15 and 25 lilac flowers, each about 8mm across. *Flowering season:* May-Aug. *Habitat:* Heaths, dry grassland and open woods. *Distribution:* Throughout, particularly in N of region.

1
2|3
4

1

Common Field-speedwell* *Veronica persica*

(Figwort Family)

To about 10cm tall. A common annual weed of cultivated fields, introduced in the 1820s from Asia. Straggly growth with rather triangular leaves and bright blue flowers with a pale lower lip.

Flowering season: Jan-Dec

Habitat: Cultivated areas

Distribution: Throughout, except far N. In Britain rarer in N and W Scotland.

Other species: Thyme-leaved Speedwell°, *V. serpyllifolia*, is a common perennial speedwell with oblong, shiny leaves. The flowering stems end in a cluster of small pale blue or white flowers, each between 6-8mm across, with darker veins. *Flowering season:* Apr-Sep

2

Butterwort* *Pinguicula vulgaris*

(Butterwort Family)

To 15cm tall, with rosette of yellowish green, sticky leaves, curling up at the edges (insect traps). Flowers solitary, long-stalked. Corolla with spur, 1.5-2.5cm long, violet, lower lip with white spots.

Flowering season: May-Jul

Habitat: Fens, bogs stream sides, flush communities

Distribution: Throughout, but commoner in mountains and the N. Also Siberia, Caucasus, N Africa, N America.

Similar species: Pale Butterwort°, *P. lusitanica*, has pale pink flowers. W fringe of Europe, including Ireland and parts of W Britain.
Alpine Butterwort, *P. alpina*, has white flowers with yellow spots on lower lip. Arctic and mountains of C Europe. Extinct in Scotland

3

Slender Speedwell* *Veronica filiformis*

(Figwort Family)

About 5cm tall. Another introduced species. Now common, especially in lawns, where its abundant flowers can form pale blue patches in spring. Large, lilac-blue flowers on very thin stems. Fruit rarely forms.

Flowering season: Mar-Jul

Habitat: Lawns, gardens, grass verges and grazed meadows

Distribution: Scattered throughout, mainly in N. Native of Caucasus.

4

Devil's-bit Scabious* *Succisa pratensis*

(Teasel Family)

To about 80cm tall, with softly hairy stem. Basal leaves broadly lanceolate, stem leaves stalkless. Flowering heads about 2cm across, compact, and violet-blue. Lanceolate bracts. Calyx has bristly teeth.

Flowering season: Jul-Sep

Habitat: Fens, meadows, poor grassland

Distribution: Europe, Siberia, NW Africa.

CALYX

1|2

3

4

1

Harebell* ❀ *Campanula rotundifolia*

(Bellflower Family)

To 50cm tall, with stalked, rounded kidney-shaped basal leaves, these usually dried out by flowering time. Stem leaves linear and lower stem finely hairy. Flower buds upright, corolla bell-shaped. Known as Bluebell in Scotland.

Flowering season: Jun-Sep

Habitat: Meadows, dry grassland, rocks

Distribution: Most of Europe, except Mediterranean.

Similar species: C. cochleariifolia ❀ is smaller (about 15cm) and has broader, toothed leaves and drooping flower buds. Mainly in the mountains. In Britian a garden escape only.

BASAL LEAVES
Harebell

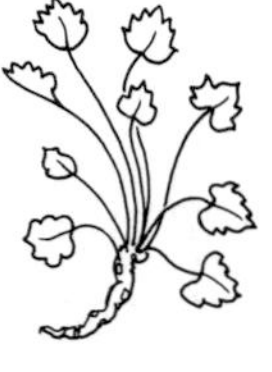

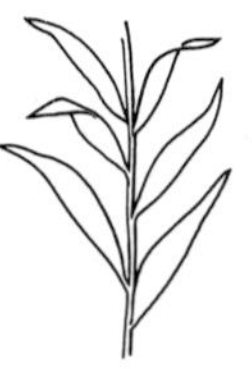

LOWER STEM LEAVES
C. cochleariifolia

Spreading Bellflower ☒ *Campanula patula*

(Bellflower Family)

To 70cm, with upright stem, branched at the top. Basal leaves spoon-shaped and stalked. Stem leaves unstalked and narrowly lanceolate. Flowers in loose cluster, somewhat drooping. Corolla funnel-shaped, and divided to the middle. Calyx teeth shorter than corolla tube.

Flowering season: Jun-Aug

Habitat: Meadows, paths scrub

Distribution: Most of Europe, but scarcer in N and W. Very local in Britain.

3

Clustered Bellflower* ❀ *Campanula glomerata*

(Bellflower Family)

To 50cm, softly hairy. Lower stem leaves long, stalked; basal leaves heart-shaped or rounded; upper stem leaves smaller and unstalked. Flowers in dense cluster at end of stem or in axils on upper half of stem. Corolla to 4cm long, violet-blue. Calyx teeth triangular.

Flowering season: Jun-Sep

Habitat: Dry hay-meadows, dry grassland, edges of woods

Distribution: Most of Europe. In Britain commonest on chalk and limestone in S and E. Absent from Ireland.

1
2|3

1 Peach-leaved Bellflower ❀

(Bellflower Family) *Campanula persicifolia*

To about 1m, mostly hairless. Basal leaves broadly lanceolate, upper leaves narrower. Flowers in loose clusters. Corolla a broad bell, up to 4cm long. *Flowering season:* Jun-Sep. *Habitat:* Open, warm woodland, scrub, woodland edges *Distribution:* Most of Europe, except extreme N and W. Introduced into Britain, mainly in S England. *Similar species:* Giant Bellflower*, *C. latifolia*, is a woodland species with large blue-purple flowers about 4cm long. Mainly Britain (especially N), Scandinavia and NE Europe.

2 Nettle-leaved Bellflower* *Campanula trachelium*

(Bellflower Family)

Stiffly hairy plant with angled stems, growing to 1m tall. Lower leaves long-stalked, heart-shaped and twice toothed (resemble nettle leaves). Stem leaves lanceolate and unstalked. Corolla a dark blue narrow bell, 3-4cm long, hairy at margin. Calyx teeth triangular. Fruit capsule with stiff hairs. *Flowering season:* Jul-Sep. *Habitat:* Open deciduous woods, scrub, hedgerows *Distribution:* Europe, N Africa, Turkey, Caucasus. In Britain mainly in S and E. *Similar species:* Creeping Bellflower*, *C. rapunculoides*, has spreading or reflexed calyx teeth, and the flowers all droop over to one side. Drier sites. Naturalized in Britain and parts of Ireland.

3 Large Venus's Looking-glass ☒

(Bellflower Family) *Legousia speculum-veneris*

Annual, branched plant to 40cm tall. Leaves lanceolate, toothed, lower ones stalked, upper unstalked. Corolla to 2.5cm across, open violet, with broad lobes. Calyx teeth narrow and pointed.
Flowering season: Jun-Aug. *Habitat:* Cultivated and waste land, vineyards *Distribution:* Most of Europe, but rarer towards N. N Africa, SW Asia. In Britain as rare introduction only.

4 Sheep's-bit* *Jasione montana*

(Bellflower Family)

To about 80cm tall, without runners. Stem has long, wavy-edged leaves in lower part only. Pale blue flowers in dense clustered heads, about 2-3cm across. Corolla to 15mm long, deeply cut into 5 parts.
Flowering season: Jun-Aug. *Habitat:* Dry grassland, dry pine woods, rocky outcrops. In Britain rather coastal. *Distribution:* Most of Europe except far N. In Britain and Ireland commonest in W.

5 Round-headed Rampion* ❀ ☒

(Bellflower Family) *Phyteuma orbiculare*

To 40cm. Basal leaves stalked, and rounded or heart-shaped, toothed. Stem leaves narrower, upper ones stalkless. Blue flowers in dense heads to about 2.5cm across. Corolla tubes curved over towards each other in bud, opening out in full flower. *Flowering season:* May-Aug *Habitat:* Dry grassland, open woodland; on chalk or limestone. *Distribution:* C Europe, with outlier in S England.

1|2
3
4|5

1

Perennial Aster ❀ *Aster amellus*

(Daisy Family)

Hairy plant, growing to 80cm. Basal leaves broadly lanceolate, stalked. Upper stem leaves long and unstalked. Flower heads 2-3cm across. Ray florets blue-violet; disc florets yellow. Fruits with pappus.
Flowering season: Aug-Oct
Habitat: Dry grassland, scrub, open woods; calcareous soils
Distribution: Mainland Europe, from C France south and eastwards. Garden plant only in British Isles.

2

Cornflower* ❀ ☒ *Centaurea cyanus*

(Daisy Family)

Annual, growing to about 80cm. Leaves narrow, the lower ones sometimes divided. Solitary blue flower heads – outer florets blue and inner florets reddish. Bracts green with black triangular markings and fringed margins. Corollas broaden towards outside of flower head.
Flowering season: Jun-Oct. *Habitat:* A weed of grain crops and waste ground.
Distribution: Europe. Has declined throughout region. Now virtually extinct in the wild in Britain, but often grown in gardens.

3

Perennial Cornflower* ❀ *Centaurea montana*

(Daisy Family)

Downy plant to 80cm, with winged stem. Leaves ovate to lanceolate, lower ones sometimes lobed. Flower heads to 5cm across and blue or pinkish-blue. Bracts with dark brown edges. Inner florets asymmetrical, violet; outer florets larger and blue.
Flowering season: May-Aug. *Habitat:* Meadows, scrub and woods; calcareous soils
Distribution: C Europe, especially mountains. Casual garden escape in Britain.

4

Blue Lettuce *Lactuca perennis*

(Daisy Family)

Hairless, growing to about 60cm. Leaves blue-green, deeply divided. Stem leaves with 2 round lobes encircling the stem. Corollas all ray form and bluish-purple. Fruits 1-1.5cm long, black, rough, with pale beak. Involucre cylindrical.
Flowering season: May-Jul. *Habitat:* Rocky outcrops, walls, footpaths
Distribution: Europe, from Belgium, C Germany and Carpathians southwards. Not in British Isles.

5

Chicory* ❀ *Cichorium intybus*

(Daisy Family)

To 1.5m with branched stem. Basal leaves lanceolate, mostly deeply divided; stem leaves small. Flower heads 3-5cm across, corollas all of ray type and pale blue. Involucre cylindrical; outer bracts short and sticking out, inner ones upright. Fruit with short pappus.
Flowering season: Jul-Oct. *Habitat:* Roadsides and waste places, pasture; chalky soils. *Distribution:* Most of Europe, except far N. Frequent in England and Wales, but rare in Scotland and Ireland.

1|2

3

4|5

1 Scottish Asphodel* *Tofieldia pusilla*

(Lily Family)

To 20cm, hairless, with basal, linear leaves. Flower head is a spike, with 5-10 small, white or greenish flowers.
Flowering season: Jun-Aug
Habitat: Bogs and flushes, mainly mountain areas
Distribution: Northern Europe (Scandinavia and Iceland), with outliers in Scotland and N England (Teesdale), and in the Alps.
Similar species: German Asphodel, *T. calyculata*, is larger, with yellowish flowers. Mainly in the Alps.

2 Yellow Star-of-Bethlehem* *Gagea lutea*

(Lily Family)

To 30cm with 1 to 6-flowered stem. Single pointed basal leaf, 5-15mm wide; lower stem leaf not overtopping flowers. Flower stalk leafless, flowers yellow, with 6 open star-like petals; 6 stamens. Ovary superior.
Flowering season: Apr-May
Habitat: Deciduous woods, orchards, scrub
Distribution: Most of Europe; Caucasus; E to Himalaya and Japan. In Britain commonest in N and C England. Absent from Ireland.
Similar species: Meadow Gagea, *G. pratensis*, has a flat basal leaf, 2-6mm wide, and lowest stem leaf overtops flowers. Meadows, fields, vineyards. C Europe, N to S Sweden. Not in British Isles.

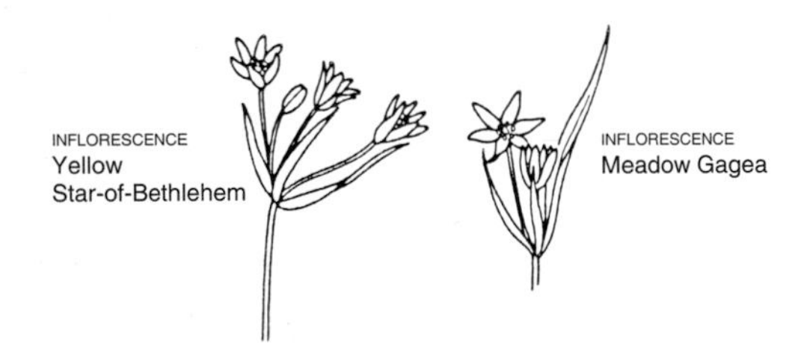

3 Bog Asphodel* *Narthecium ossifragum*

(Lily Family)

To 30cm, hairless, with upright stem. Leaves sword-shaped, arranged in 2 rows, the upper becoming increasingly smaller towards inflorescence. Flowers long-stalked, arranged in a loose raceme. Perianth segments 6, outer ones green inner ones yellow, closing up with age. Anthers dark orange, with woolly hairs. Ovary superior. Fruit a narrow, pointed capsule.
Flowering season: Jul-Aug
Habitat: Acid bogs, flushes and wet heaths
Distribution: Atlantic. W Europe, from Spain and W France to Ireland, Britain, Holland, N Germany and Scandinavia.

1|2
3

1

Daffodil* ❀ *Narcissus pseudonarcissus*

(Daffodil Family)

Hairless, often blue-green plant, to 40cm tall. Leaves all basal and grass-like, fleshy and to 15mm across. Flowers scented and usually solitary. Central deep yellow and wavy-edged "trumpet" to about 3cm long, surrounded by 6 pale yellow perianth segments. Flowers arise from a yellowish-green perianth tube, with a papery leaf at its base. Flowers 5-10cm across; 6 stamens; ovary inferior (below the rest of flower), unlike members of the lily family. 1 style with 3 stigmas. Fruit a tripartite capsule.

Flowering season: Mar-Apr

Habitat: Meadows, woods, scrub, on acid, humus rich soils

Distribution: Mainly western and local, from Spain to Britain, E to Vosges and Lake Constance area, SE to Venice. Often planted and escaped (also many garden forms).

2

Yellow Iris (Yellow Flag)* ❀ *Iris pseudacorus*

(Iris Family)

Hairless plant to more than 1m tall. Leaves sword-shaped, to 3cm across, shorter than stem and arranged in 2 rows. Stem rounded, with several flowers, sometimes covered by a leaf. Flowers yellow, the 3 outermost perianth segments 5-10cm long, lacking upright hairs, 3 inner ones not longer than stigmas; 3 stamens; inferior ovary. 1 style with 3 petal-like, 2-lipped stigmas. Fruit a tripartite capsule.

Flowering season: Jun-Sep

Habitat: Banks, ditches, reed-beds; rich, muddy soils, often in sites subject to flooding

Distribution: Most of Europe, Asia, NW Africa.

Note: In all other Iris species of the region the inner perianth segments are noticeably longer than the stigmas. This is true of the blue-flowered species and for the very rare yellow flowered *Iris variegata* ❀. The latter has a line of upright hairs along the upper surface of the outer perianth segments, and brown veins (Bearded Iris).

FLOWER
Iris variegata

FLOWER
Yellow Iris

1

2

1 Lady's-slipper (Orchid)* ❀ ☒

(Orchid Family) *Cypripedium calceolus*

About 70cm tall, often with more than 1 stem. Stem with short hairs and 3-5 broad oval, strongly veined leaves, often sheathing stem. Flowers solitary or up to 5. Each has 2 outer and 2 inner rather narrow reddish-brown perianth segments. The lip ("slipper") is 3-4cm long, rounded at the front, inflated, yellow, with reddish spots and stripes inside.
Flowering season: May-Jul
Habitat: Shady sites on calcareous soils
Distribution: C and N Europe, widespread, but local and often rare. From Lappland to N Italy and from the Pyrenees to NE Asia. In Britain extremely rare and totally protected.

2 Birthwort* ☠ ☒ *Aristolochia clematitis*

(Birthwort Family)

To 1m tall, with upright, unbranched stem. Leaves heart-shaped, about as long as broad, with obvious veins spreading out from leaf-stalk. Flowers in clusters in the leaf axils, erect when opened. Perianth zygomorphic, 3-5cm long, yellow, inflated towards base and narrowing to a lipped tube at the top. Fruit a hanging, somewhat pear-shaped capsule.
Flowering season: May-Jun
Habitat: Open woodland, scrub, walls, vineyards
Distribution: Central Europe, Mediterranean, Turkey, Caucasus. In Britain rare and scattered (introduced).

3 Yellow Water-lily* ❀ *Nuphar lutea*

(Water-lily Family)

Water plant with broad, oval, wavy-edged floating leaves to 30cm long. Leaf stalks up to 2m long (depending on water depth). Flowers 3-5cm across, usually with 5-6 rounded yellow or orange sepals, surrounding many (up to 20) smaller petals and many stamens. Ovary superior, with shield-shaped stigma, with 15-20 radial brown stripes. Fruit pear-shaped, 2-4cm long.
Flowering season: Jun-Aug
Habitat: In rich standing or slow-flowing water, to about 3m depth, with muddy bottom
Distribution: Europe, E to Lake Baikal, S to N Africa; Turkey and Caucasus.
Similar species: Least Water-lily*, *N. pumila*, has smaller flowers (to 4cm across) and leaves (to 10cm long). Stigma disc has wavy edge, and 8-10 radial brown stripes. Rare in C Europe and England; local in N and C Scotland.

STIGMATIC SURFACE OF OVARY
Least Water lily

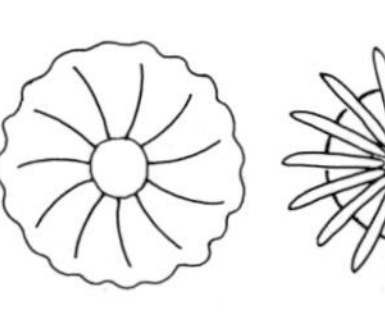

STIGMATIC SURFACE OF OVARY
Yellow Water lily

1|2
3

1

Marsh Marigold* ❀ *Caltha palustris*

(Buttercup Family)

Hairless plant, to 50cm tall. Leaves broad, shiny, toothed and heart-shaped with long stalks. Upper stem leaves similar, but smaller and unstalked. Flowers bright shiny yellow, to 5cm across. Fruits to 2.5cm long, in a star-shaped cluster.

Flowering season: Mar-Jul

Habitat: Stream sides, wet meadows and wet woodland

Distribution: Europe, N Asia, America.

FRUIT

2

Globeflower* ❀ *Trollius europaeus*

(Buttercup Family)

To 70cm tall. Lower leaves stalked and palmate, with toothed lobes; stem leaves unstalked and 3-lobed. Flowers pale or golden yellow, to 3cm across, rounded in shape. Fruit to 1.5cm long and beaked.

Flowering season: Apr-Jul

Habitat: Wet meadows, scrub, mountain woods, tall herb communities

Distribution: Most of Europe. Only in mountains in the S. Asia, N America. Mainly in N and W of Britain and Ireland.

FRUIT

3

Yellow Pheasant's-eye ☠ ❀ *Adonis vernalis*

(Buttercup Family)

To 50cm. Leaves all stalked and feathery, with pointed tips. Flowers solitary, yellow, to about 7cm across. Sepals broadly oval and hairy. Petals (10-20) long and oval, sometimes toothed at end and golden yellow. Fruits (nutlets) to 5mm, hairy with hooked beak.

Flowering season: Apr-May

Habitat: Heathy grassland, open pine woods, mainly on calcareous, but also on sandy soils

Distribution: From Spain to Sweden, reaching SE Europe and Urals. Rare in C Europe. Absent from British Isles.

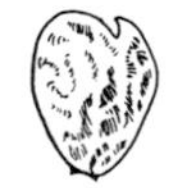

FRUIT

4

Yellow Anemone* ❀ *Anemone ranunculoides*

(Buttercup Family)

To 30cm tall, hairless plant. Basal leaves over by flowering time. 3 short-stalked palmate, divided leaves on upper stem. Lobes irregularly and rather coarsely toothed. Flowers 2-3cm across, flower stalks crinkled and hairy. 5-6 yellow perianth segments (petaloid sepals), hairy on outsides. Fruits small, densely covered in short, straight bristly hairs.

Flowering season: Mar-May

Habitat: Mixed deciduous woods, especially wet river-valley woods, hedges, on moist, humus-rich soils

Distribution: Most of Europe, from N Spain, C Italy to S Scandinavia. Rarely naturalized in Britain.

1
2|3
4

1

Lesser Celandine* ❀ *Ranunculus ficaria*

(Buttercup Family)

Hairless plant growing to 30cm tall, with creeping stems, rooting at nodes. Leaves heart-shaped and fleshy, with wavy margins and long stalks. May have bulbils in axils of stem leaves. Flowers yellow (fading to white) 2-3cm across, with 3 to 7 sepals and 8 to 12 long petals. Fruits are hairy achenes, with straight beak.

Flowering season: Mar-May

Habitat: Deciduous woods, scrub, damp meadows

Distribution: Europe, except Iceland and much of Scandinavia; N Africa, Asia, Caucasus.

2

Creeping Buttercup* *Ranunculus repens*

(Buttercup Family)

To 50cm, with leafy, rooting runners. Basal leaves 3-lobed, with stalked middle lobe (distinctive feature). Flowers 2-3cm across, with furrowed stalks. Sepals hairy and close to petals. Achenes 2.5-3.5mm long, bare, with short beak.

Flowering season: May-Aug

Habitat: Woods, scrub, meadows, farmland, footpaths, wasteland

Distribution: Europe, Asia, N Africa; dispersed almost all over the world.

3

Lesser Spearwort* *Ranunculus flammula*

(Buttercup Family)

To 70cm tall, usually much-branched. Leaves narrowly elliptical to narrowly lanceolate. Flowers to 1.5cm across. Achenes round, about 1mm long, smooth, with short, straight beak.

Flowering season: May-Sep

Habitat: Ditches, damp meadows, fens, flushes

Distribution: Most of Europe, E to Caucasus and Urals; Asia, N America.

4

Bulbous Buttercup* *Ranunculus bulbosus*

(Buttercup Family)

To 40cm, hairy plant with stem base swollen below ground. Basal leaves 3-lobed and stalked. Flowers 2-3cm across, bright yellow, with stalks furrowed. Sepals turn back from the flower, along the stems.

Flowering season: May-Jun

Habitat: Likes drier pastures than the other 2 common buttercups (Creeping B. and Meadow B.). Prefers lime-rich soils

Distribution: Much of Europe. Common throughout England and most of Wales; scattered in Scotland and Ireland.

1|2
3
4

1 Meadow Buttercup* *Ranunculus acris*

(Buttercup Family)

To 1m tall, softly hairy to hairless plant with branched stem. Basal leaves (3) 5 to 7-lobed, each lobe further divided into 3. Stem leaves less divided and with shorter stalks. Flowers to 3cm across, on unfurrowed stalks. Sepals upright. Achenes rounded, hairless, with slightly curved beak.

ACHENE

Flowering season: May-Sep
Habitat: Meadows, pasture, edges of footpaths
Distribution: Europe, Asia N to Himalaya, N Africa, spread throughout the world.

2 Common Meadow-rue* *Thalictrum flavum*

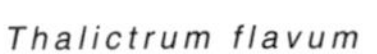

(Buttercup Family)

Almost hairless, growing to 2 m, with ridged stem. Lower leaves stalked, upper leaves unstalked, all 2 to 3-times pinnately divided, terminal leaflet toothed. Leaflets ovate in outline, longer than broad, wedge-shaped and narrowing, dark green above, pale green beneath. Inflorescence branched, yellow; flowers upright, scented, with 4 lanceolate, whitish sepals which fall off early, revealing the many upright, yellow stamens. Achenes rounded and ribbed, 1.5-2.5mm long, with reddish-brown remains of the stigma.

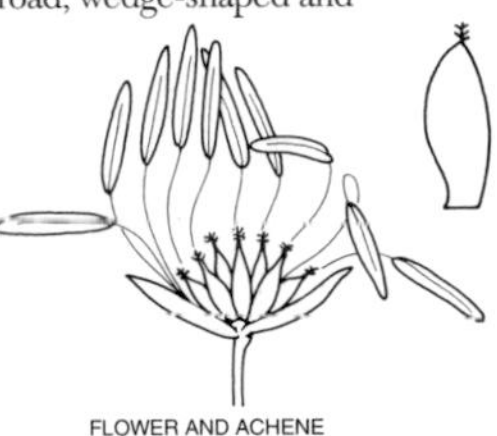
FLOWER AND ACHENE

Flowering season: Jun-Aug
Habitat: Damp meadows, fens
Distribution: Europe; Asia.

3 Greater Celandine* ☠ *Chelidonium majus*

(Poppy Family)

To 1m tall. Stem upright, branched, with bristly hairs and bright orange milky sap. Leaves green above, blue-green beneath, pinnate, with oval, toothed lobes. Flowers yellow, 2-3cm across; 2 sepals, falling off at flowering time. Petals 4, equal and oval. Stamens numerous, anthers club-shaped. Ovary superior. Fruit a 2-5cm long capsule.
Flowering season: May-Oct
Habitat: Waste ground, footpaths, walls, scrub, open woods and parks
Distribution: Most of Europe, except far N. Introduced in many areas, including most if not all of Britain and Ireland. Asia, N Africa.

1|2

3

1

Hedge Mustard*

Sisymbrium officinale

(Cabbage Family)

Shortly hairy plant to 80cm tall. Basal leaves pinnate and stalked; stem leaves smaller, unstalked. Flowers stalked, without bracts. Sepals upright 1-1.5mm long; petals 2-4mm long. Fruits upright, closely pressed to stem, lacking beak, 1-2cm long, about 1mm wide, each valve with 3 ribs.

Flowering season: May-Oct

Habitat: Rocks, walls, waste ground

Distribution: Most of Europe.

2

Winter-cress*

Barbarea vulgaris

(Cabbage Family)

Hairless plant, to 80cm tall. Basal leaves pinnate with the rounded terminal lobe the largest. Stem leaves undivided and coarsely toothed. Flowers stalked and without bracts. Sepals upright, 2.5-3.5mm long; petals 5-7mm long. Fruits rectangular in cross-section, unbeaked, 15-25mm long, each valve with obvious central rib.

Flowering season: May-Aug

Habitat: Waste ground, river banks, footpaths

Distribution: Most of Europe; Asia. In Britain and Ireland throughout lowlands, but less common in N.

3

Charlock*

Sinapis arvensis

(Cabbage Family)

To about 80cm tall, a common weed with bright yellow flowers. Leaves hairy and toothed or lobed, the upper stalkless and undivided. Fruit a siliqua with straight tips, not curved as in White Mustard.

Flowering season: May-Jul

Habitat: Cereal crops and field margins, especially on chalky or heavy soils.

Distribution: Throughout

Similar species: White Mustard*, *S. alba*, is similar to Charlock, but its leaves are more deeply lobed (see p 48).

Rape*, *Brassica napus*, is a common escape from cultivation. About 1m tall, with larger yellow flowers.

4

Yellow Whitlowgrass* ❀ ☒

Draba aizoides

(Cabbage Family)

To about 10cm, growing in loose cushions. Leaves evergreen, narrow, fringed with stiff bristles. Stem leafless. Sepals 3-4mm long, hairless. Petals 4-6mm long. Fruit 6-10mm long, elongate and hairless silicula.

Flowering season: Apr-Aug

Habitat: Rocks, scree, open grassland on calcareous soils

Distribution: Mountains of C and S Europe. Rare plant in Britain, confined to S Wales.

SILICULA

1|2

3

4

1

Treacle Mustard* *Erysimum cheiranthoides*

(Cabbage Family)

To about 1m, with long, narrow leaves; plant covered in branched hairs. Small, yellow flowers (to about 6mm across), arranged in clusters. Petals about twice as long as sepals. Fruit an upright siliqua, with square cross-section, 1-5cm long.

Flowering season: Jun-Sep

Habitat: Arable fields and waste land

Distribution: Most of Europe, except much of S. In Britain mainly in E England.

2

Ball Mustard* *Neslia paniculata*

(Cabbage Family)

To 80cm tall, branched only towards top. Lower stem and leaves with rough, stellate hairs. Leaves lanceolate, lower ones stalked, upper ones unstalked and with arrow-shaped base.

Sepals erect, about 1.5mm long, yellow-green. Petals 2-2.5mm long, rounded and bright yellow. Fruit round and wrinkled, 1.5-2mm long.

Flowering season: May-Aug

Habitat: Fields, footpaths, waste ground, walls, embankments

Distribution: Most of Europe; W Asia, N Africa. Rather uncommon; in Britain a rare casual.

FRUIT
Ball Mustard

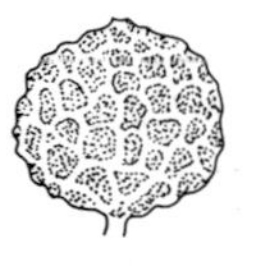

FRUIT
Woad

3

Woad* *Isatis tinctoria*

(Cabbage Family)

To 1m tall, rather bluish-green plant, softly hairy at base, but hairless in upper stem. Leaves entire, or somewhat arrow-shaped, rarely toothed, with wide white midrib above. Basal leaves stalked, dying off towards flowering period. Stem leaves unstalked, 2-6cm long and often clasping stem with auricles. Inflorescence branched, with very thin flower stalks, arching downwards soon after flowering. Sepals 1.5-2mm long, persisting after flowering; petals 3-4mm long, yellow. Fruit elliptical to obovate, drooping, 8-25mm long, 3-7mm wide, becoming blackish on ripening, with broad wings.

Flowering season: May-Jul

Habitat: Rocks, walls, railway embankments, vineyards, farmland, river banks

Distribution: In Europe mainly C and S, scattered. Asia, N Africa. In Britain rare and local, mainly in S England.

1

2|3

1 Great Yellow-cress* *Rorippa amphibia*

(Cabbage Family)

Mainly hairless plant growing to about 1.5m tall. Leaves variable, entire or shallowly lobed and toothed. Sepals erect, 2mm long. Petals 4-5mm long, yellow. Fruits elongate, 3-7mm long, on horizontal or drooping stems.
Flowering season: May-Aug
Habitat: River banks, wet meadows, ditches
Distribution: Europe, N Asia. In Britain mainly in lowland England and E Wales.

2 Perennial Wall-rocket* *Diplotaxis tenuifolia*

(Cabbage Family)

Hairless plant about 60cm tall with bluish stems. Leaves mostly deeply pinnate. Sepals 4-5mm long, the outer 2 horizontal, inner 2 almost vertical. Petals 8-15mm long, yellow. Fruit long-stemmed, 2.5-3.5cm long, about 2mm wide. Seeds arranged in 2 rows.
Flowering season: May-Oct
Habitat: Waste land, walls, footpaths, fields
Distribution: Most of Europe, except N; Asia; N Africa. In Britain mainly in SE and probably not native.

3 White Mustard* *Sinapis alba*

(Cabbage Family)

To 80cm tall, hairy below. Leaves stalked, lobed or pinnate, narrower towards top of plant. Sepals 4-6mm long; petals 7-10mm long, yellow. Fruits erect to horizontal, 2.5-4cm long, with obvious beak and many long, stiff hairs.
Flowering season: Jun-Oct
Habitat: Arable land, waste ground, footpaths.
Distribution: Europe, except extreme N.

4 Wild Mignonette* *Reseda lutea*

(Mignonette Family)

Hairless plant growing to 80cm tall. Leaves 3-lobed or pinnate, with wavy margins. Flower stalks to 5mm long. Usually 6 elongate sepals, 2-3mm long. Petals 6, yellowish, the upper pair 4-5mm long, and 3-lobed. Stamens numerous. Capsule 10-12mm long, elongate and 3-pointed.
Flowering season: May-Oct
Habitat: Waste ground, footpath and field margins
Distribution: Europe, Mediterranean. In Britain mainly in the E half.
Similar species: Weld*, *R. luteola*, grows to 1.5m, has linear, entire leaves, 4 sepals and petals, and a rounded capsule.

FLOWER
Wild Mignonette

1|2
3
4

1

Biting Stonecrop*

Sedum acre

(Stonecrop Family)

Hairless mat-forming plant to 15cm tall. Non-flowering stems with thick covering of oval, fleshy leaves. Leaves flat-topped, rounded below, to 4mm long, and sharp-tasting. Flowers 5-partite. Sepals short and oval, about 3mm long. Petals lanceolate, pointed, almost horizontal and 7-10mm long, yellow. Stamens 10. Follicles spreading in star-shape, 3-5mm long.

Flowering season: Jun-Aug

Habitat: Rocks, dry grassland, walls, waste ground

Distribution: Most of Europe; N Africa; Asia.

LEAF

Tasteless Stonecrop Biting Stonecrop

Similar species: Tasteless Stonecrop°, *S. sexangulare*, has no sharp taste. Leaves cylindrical, to 6mm long, 1mm thick, with short spur at base. Mainland Europe, naturalized in a few places in Britain.

2

Reflexed Stonecrop* ❀

Sedum reflexum

(Stonecrop Family)

To 40cm tall, with low-growing mat-forming, rooting stems. Leaves fleshy and narrow, blue or blue-green, 1-2cm long, 2-3mm wide, almost rounded and slightly pointed, with short spur. Flowers mostly 5-partite; sepals narrowly oval, pointed, 3-6mm long; petals lanceolate, 5-10mm long; stamens 10, anthers with long hairs at base. Fruit a head of pointed follicles, 5-7mm long.

Flowering season: Jun-Aug

Habitat: Walls, dry slopes, rocks, open woodland; on lime-poor soils.

Distribution: Most of Europe, N to S Scandinavia. Naturalized in Britain.

Similar species: Rock Stonecrop°, *S. forsterianum*, is very similar, but its leaves are flat on the top. W Europe, including SW England and Wales.

3

Alternate-leaved Golden-saxifrage*

(Saxifrage Family)

Chrysosplenium alternifolium

To 20cm tall, loose-growing plant with runners fanning out at surface of ground. Leaves with long stalks, rounded and heart-shaped, shiny, almost hairless, with blunt teeth. Basal leaves in a rosette-like arrangement; stem leaves alternate. Flowers small, greenish-yellow, surrounded by many yellowish leaves. 4 sepals, no petals; usually 8 stamens. Capsule cup-shaped and opening before the fruits are fully ripe.

Flowering season: Apr-Jun

Habitat: Flushes, stream sides, shady woods, scrub, tall herb communities.

Distribution: Europe, except extreme S; Caucasus. Absent from Ireland and extreme W of Britain, and local elsewhere.

Similar species: Opposite-leaved Golden-saxifrage°, *C. oppositifolium*, has rectangular stem, opposite stem leaves and basal leaves not heart-shaped. Commoner in Britain than previous species.

FLOWER

Alternate-leaved Golden-saxifrage

1|2
3

1 Agrimony* *Agrimonia eupatoria*

(Rose Family)

Upright plant, to 1.5m tall, covered with soft hairs. Leaves pinnate, the larger leaflets having smaller leaflets between them. Leaflets toothed. Flowers yellow, on very short stalks. Receptacle goblet-shaped, with 10 longitudinal furrows, with hooked bristles. Petals narrowly obovate, 4-6mm long. Fruit nodding.

Flowering season: Jun-Sep

Habitat: Open woods, hedges, meadows; usually on calcareous soils

Distribution: Most of Europe. Rare in N Scotland.

Similar species: Fragrant Agrimony°, *A. procera*, has aromatic glands on the stems and leaves. Fruit slightly ridged.

FRUIT
Agrimony

2 Silverweed* *Potentilla anserina*

(Rose Family)

Hairy plant to 15cm tall, with long, creeping stems, rooting at the nodes. Basal leaves to 20cm long, pinnate, with toothed leaflets. Leaflets almost smooth above, silvery hairy beneath. Flowers solitary and long-stalked, with 5 petals, borne in leaf-axils, and 2-3cm across. Epicalyx silkily hairy, segments often toothed. Sepals of equal length, pointed, mostly undivided.

Flowering season: May-Sep

Habitat: Meadows, footpath edges, waste land

Distribution: Almost worldwide.

3 Tormentil* *Potentilla erecta*

(Rose Family)

Hairy plant, to 30cm tall. Basal leaves usually over by flowering time. Stem leaves trifoliate, but appearing 5-digitate because of leaflet-like stipules. Leaflets toothed from middle onwards. Flowers stalked, mostly with 4 petals, about 1cm across. Epicalyx present. Sepals mostly shorter and broader. Petals a little longer than sepals.

Flowering season: May-Oct

Habitat: Meadows, bogs, heaths

Distribution: Europe; Asia; N Africa.

4 Creeping Cinquefoil* *Potentilla reptans*

(Rose Family)

To 20cm, spreading by means of long runners. The flowers are large (to 2.5cm across) and yellow, with 5 petals. The compound leaves have 5 narrow leaflets attached centrally, hence the common name, from the French.

Flowering season: Jun-Sep

Habitat: Hedges, banks, roadsides, grassland, waste places, mainly on neutral or alkaline soils

Distribution: Throughout, but rare in C and N Scotland, and scattered in N Ireland.

1
2
3|4

1

Broom*☠ *Cytisus scoparius*

(Pea Family)

Branched shrub, to 2m tall. Stems mostly upright, with green leaves; stem 5-angled and mostly bare (young stems have appressed hairs). Leaves trifoliate and stalked on older stems, stalkless and simple on young stems. Leaflets elliptical or obovate, to 2cm long, dark green, bare or with appressed hairs. Flowers delicately scented, solitary or paired in leaf axils. Flower stalk twice as long as the short, bell-shaped, 2-lipped calyx. Cleft between the 2 lips much deeper than that in upper lip. Corolla golden yellow, 1.5-2cm long; all petals of similar length. Fruit to over 4cm long, flat, hairy at edges, otherwise bare, black when ripe.
Flowering season: May-Jun
Habitat: Heaths, clearings, scrub; often planted by roads; avoids calcareous soils
Distribution: W, S and C Europe, becoming rarer towards E and N (frost sensitive).

2

Common Gorse* *Ulex europaeus*

(Pea Family)

Bushy, spiny shrub to about 2m tall. Stems have furrowed, hairless terminal spines up to 2.5cm long. Flowers pale yellow, up to 2cm across, with a distinct smell of coconut.
Flowering season: Jan-Dec, but mainly in spring
Habitat: Heath, poor grassland; mainly on acid soils
Distribution: Atlantic – common in Britain, Ireland, Holland, NW France.
Similar species: Dwarf Gorse*, *U. minor*, is smaller, with deeper yellow flowers and smaller spines. Britain and W France.
Western Gorse*, *U. gallii*, is similar, but with more rigid spines. Flowers in late summer and autumn.

1

2

1

Dyer's Greenweed* *Genista tinctoria*

(Pea Family)

Sparsely hairy plant to 1m tall, with erect spineless twigs. Leaves lanceolate. Calyx 2-lipped; cleft between the 2 lips no deeper than that in upper lip. Corolla 10-15mm long. Fruit 1.5-3cm long, usually hairless.
Flowering season: Jun-Sep
Habitat: Heaths, pastures, scrub, open woods
Distribution: Most of Europe, except N Scandinavia; Asia.

2

Wild Liquorice* *Astragalus glycyphyllos*

(Pea Family)

Robust plant with virtually hairless stems, growing to 1m tall. Leaves pinnate with terminal leaflet; leaflets to 3cm long. Corolla 1.1-1.6cm long, with blunt keel. Fruit stalked, linear, to 4cm long, somewhat inflated when ripe, hairless, rather curved.
Flowering season: Jun-Aug
Habitat: Scrub, woodland edges, footpaths, rocky outcrops
Distribution: Most of Europe, rarer in N, mainly in mountains in S. Scattered through England and S Scotland. Absent from Ireland.

3

Yellow Milk-vetch* ☒ *Oxytropis campestris*

(Pea Family)

Sparsely hairy, tufted plant to 20cm. Leaves pinnate with terminal leaflet. Inflorescence long-stalked with several flowers in dense heads; corolla 1.5-2cm long, pale yellow; keel with tooth-like points. Fruit inflated, erect, thickly hairy.
Flowering season: Jun-Aug
Habitat: Grassland, often calcareous
Distribution: Mountains of S and C Europe, N and S Scandinavia. Outlier in Scotland (rare).

4

Ribbed (Common) Melilot* *Melilotus officinalis*

(Pea Family)

Erect plant with trifoliate leaves, growing to 1.5m. Leaflets with toothed margins, central leaflet longer stalked than others. Flowers drooping. Corolla 5.5-7mm long, yellow. Fruit 3-4mm long, ovate, hairless, with cross furrows.
Flowering season: May-Oct
Habitat: Margins of footpaths and fields, waste ground
Distribution: Europe; Asia.

5

Meadow Vetchling* *Lathyrus pratensis*

(Pea Family)

Straggling plant to 1m tall. Leaves with 1 pair of parallel-veined lanceolate leaves and a simple or branched tendril. Flowers weakly scented. Corolla to 2cm long, yellow. Fruit a blackish hairless pod, to 4cm long.
Flowering season: May-Aug
Habitat: Meadows, scrub, woodland edges
Distribution: Most of Europe; Asia; N Africa.

1|2
3
4|5

1 Hop Trefoil* *Trifolium campestre*

(Pea Family)

Hairy plant to 30cm. Leaves alternate and trifoliate, terminal leaflet longer-stalked than laterals. Yellow flowers 4-5mm long, in rounded flower heads, to 15mm across.

Flowering season: May-Oct

Habitat: Dry grassland

Distribution: Much of Europe, except N.

Similar species: Large Hop Trefoil°, *T. aureum*, is somewhat larger, with almost stalkless terminal leaflet. Mainly C, N and E Europe; only in mountains in S. In Britain introduced to SE.

2 Black Medick* *Medicago lupulina*

(Pea Family)

To 50cm tall. Basal leaves over by flowering time. Stem leaves trifoliate, terminal leaflet longer-stalked than laterals. Leaflets obovate, finely toothed at end, somewhat hairy, at least on undersides. Flowers numerous, in rounded or oval heads, 4-6mm across. Corolla 2-3.5mm long, remaining yellow after flowering, drooping. Fruit pods 3mm long, kidney-shaped, black-brown when ripe.

Flowering season: May-Oct

Habitat: Hay meadows, edges of footpaths, waste ground

Distribution: Most of Europe, spread almost worldwide.

Similar species: Lesser Hop Trefoil°, *Trifolium dubium*, is smaller, and has no central point to leaflets.

3 Kidney Vetch* *Anthyllis vulneraria*

(Pea Family)

To 50cm tall. Basal leaves simple, or with few leaflets. Stem leaves mostly pinnate; leaflets narrow, entire. Flowers in heads with 3 to 7-lobed involucre below. Calyx woolly and somewhat inflated. Corolla 1-2cm long, pale yellow to reddish. Fruit hidden within calyx.

Flowering season: May-Oct

Habitat: Rocks, poor grassland, edges of footpaths, mostly on chalk

Distribution: Europe; E to Caucasus; S to N Africa.

1|2
3

1

Small Scorpion Vetch❀ *Coronilla vaginalis*

(Pea Family)

Hairless plant to 20cm, with woody, branched low-lying stem. Leaves short-stalked with 5 to 13 blue-green, obovate, pale-edged leaflets, each to 1cm long. Stipules sheath-like, pale and almost as long as leaflets. Flowers scented and in groups of up to 10 in long-stalked inflorescence. Corolla to 1cm long; flower-stalk about as long as calyx. Fruit pods drooping, straight, furrowed, 6-sided, 4 sides with wavy ridges.

Flowering season: Jun-Aug

Habitat: Scree, grassland, open woods, on calcareous soils

Distribution: S Europe, S C Europe. Not in British Isles.

Similar species: Horseshoe Vetch*, *Hippocrepis comosa*, has narrower leaves, without pale border, and flat pods, with horseshoe-shaped segments. Common throughout, N to England, where it is restricted to chalk and limestone.

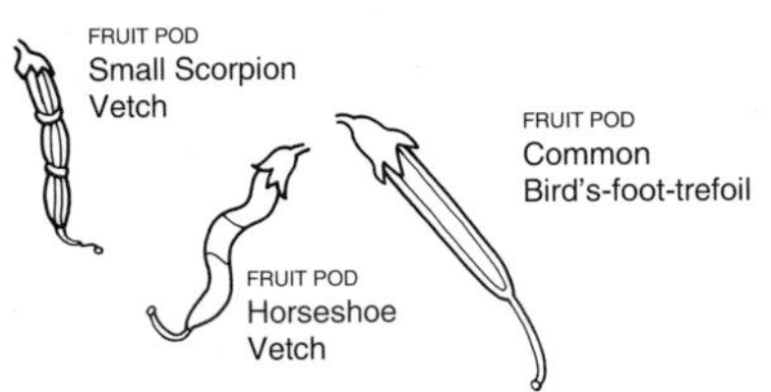

2

Common Bird's-foot-trefoil* *Lotus corniculatus*

(Pea Family)

To 40cm tall, with 5-lobed leaves, the 3 upper leaflets with short stalk, lower pair stalkless (looks trifoliate). Flowers in stalked clusters. Corolla to 1.5cm long, dark yellow, often reddish, particularly in bud. Fruits to 2cm long, rounded, straight, chestnut brown when ripe and spread out like bird's foot. Calyx teeth erect in bud.

Flowering season: May-Oct

Habitat: Dry grassland, hay meadows, edges of footpaths, open woods

Distribution: Most of Europe; Asia; N and E Africa. Common in British Isles.

3

Greater Bird's-foot-trefoil* *Lotus uliginosus*

(Pea Family)

Like a large, often hairy version of previous species, growing to 60cm, with hollow stems. Leaflets rather blue-green and oval. Inflorescences on long stalks to 15cm. Flowers pale yellow, without reddish tinge. Calyx teeth turned backwards in bud.

Flowering season: Jun-Aug

Habitat: Fens and damp grassland

Distribution: Mainly N and W Europe; absent from far N.

1
2|3

1

Cypress Spurge* *Euphorbia cyparissias*

(Spurge Family)

Hairless plant to 50cm tall, with poisonous white milky sap. Stem has up to 20 thickly-leafed non-flowering, and to 10 flowering side branches. Leaves linear, entire, to 4cm long, up to 3mm broad. Flowers very small, within cup-like glands which, together with yellow (later red) bracts, form a false flower (cyathium).
Flowering season: Apr-Jul. *Habitat:* Dry grassland, open woods
Distribution: Most of Europe, introduced to Britain and N Europe, but possibly native in parts of SE England.
Note: There are many spurge species in Europe. All have milky juice and green or yellowish inflorescences, with the characteristic false flower.

2

Hairy St John's-wort* *Hypericum hirsutum*

(St John's-wort Family)

Softly hairy plant to 1m tall. Hairs on stems and on both sides of leaves distinguish this species. Flowers pale yellow and quite large (to 1.5cm across).
Flowering season: Jul-Aug. *Habitat:* Damp woods, scrub, usually on calcareous soils
Distribution: Europe, except far N. Throughout England, rare in most of Wales, Scotland and Ireland.

3

Square-stalked St John's-wort*

(St John's-wort Family) *Hypericum tetrapterum*

Stems with 4 ridges. Flowers rather small and pale.
Flowering season: Jun-Sep *Habitat:* Wet grassland and damp woodland
Distribution: Throughout, except C and N Scotland.

4

Perforate St John's-wort* *Hypericum perforatum*

(St John's-wort Family)

Hairless plant, to 1m tall. Leaves ovate to linear, with many translucent spots. Flowers 5-partite. Sepals narrow, to 15mm long, sepals and petals sometimes with black spots. Stamens numerous, in 5 groups. 3-5 styles.
Flowering season: Jun-Sep. *Habitat:* Rocks, dry grassland, meadows, open woods
Distribution: Europe, except far N; W Asia; N Africa. In Britain throughout, but rare in C and W Scotland. Widespread in Ireland.

5

Touch-me-not Balsam* *Impatiens noli-tangere*

(Balsam Family)

Hairless plant, to 1m tall. Leaves alternate, roughly toothed. Flowers, solitary, or in groups of up to 4, in the leaf axils, on drooping stalks. Corolla about 3cm long, lip with red spots; curved, tapering spur. Fruit 2-3cm long, club-shaped capsule, exploding to release seeds when ripe.
Flowering season: Jul-Sep. *Habitat:* Damp woods, scrub, clearings
Distribution: Most of Europe; E to Japan. In Britain native only in N Wales and Lake District, introduced elsewhere.
Similar species: Small Balsam°, *I. parviflora*, is similar, but with a straight spur. Orange Balsam°, *I. capensis*, has orange flowers, spotted with brown. The larger Himalayan Balsam°, *I. glandulifera*, has purple-pink flowers and hollow, reddish stems.

1

2|3

4|5

1

Common Rock-rose* ✿

(Rock-rose Family) *Helianthemum nummularium*

Hairy dwarf shrub, to 50cm tall. Leaves opposite, linear, with stipules at base. Flowers to 3cm across. Petals obovate; sepals ovate, whitish, with obvious veins.
Flowering season: May-Sep. *Habitat:* Rocks, dry grassland
Distribution: Europe, except far N; N Africa; Turkey. Very rare in Ireland.
Similar species: Hoary Rock-rose*, *H. canum*, lacks stipules, and leaves are greyish below. Rare in Britain. P
Note: Common Rock-rose is very variable, in characters such as leaf hairiness and flower size. Many subspecies have been described, particularly from the Alps.

2

Wild Pansy* ✿

Viola tricolor

(Violet Family)

To 30cm tall, with leafy stem. Lower leaves rounded with heart-shaped base, with toothed margins. Upper leaves longer, narrowing towards base. Stipules deeply pinnate, with large, lanceolate terminal lobe. Flowers to 3cm tall, weakly fragrant. Petals much longer than calyx, yellow to blue, lower ones with dark stripes; lower lip with dark yellow spot. Spur longer than calyx.
Flowering season: Jun-Aug. *Habitat:* Waste ground, fields, meadows
Distribution: Most of Europe.
Similar species: Field Pansy*, *V. arvensis*. The terminal lobe of the stipule resembles leaf. Spur about same length as calyx; sepals at least as long as petals, which are usually pale yellow.
Note: Wild Pansy is very variable, especially in flower colour (often blue, particularly upper pair of petals).

3

Common Evening-primrose* ✿

(Willowherb Family) *Oenothera biennis*

To about 1m tall, with downy, leafy stem. Basal leaves lanceolate to obovate, narrowing towards stem, toothed or with entire margins. Stem leaves many and smaller. Flowers 2-3cm long, solitary in leaf axils. Sepals turned back, shorter than elongated ovary beneath. Petals much longer than stamens. Fruits to 3cm long, elongated and rectangular, splitting to release seeds.
Flowering season: Jun-Oct. *Habitat:* footpaths, waste ground, dunes
Distribution: Europe, except far N.
Note: There are several species of Evening-primrose, mostly introduced from N America.

4

Wild Parsnip*

Pastinaca sativa

(Carrot Family)

Rather hairy plant to 1.5m tall. Leaves pinnate, with 2-7 pairs of irregularly toothed lobes. Upper leaves often very much reduced. Flowers in umbels, lacking bracts and bracteoles. Petals yellow, even-sized, 0.5mm long, 1mm broad, and curved towards outside. Fruit flat and lentil-shaped, 5-7mm long, narrowly winged, yellow-brown when ripe.
Flowering season: Jul-Sep. *Habitat:* Meadows, footpaths, waste ground
Distribution: Most of Europe; Caucasus; Siberia. Common on chalk in England.

1
2
3|4

1

Yellow Bird's-nest* *Monotropa hypopitys*

(Wintergreen Family)

To 30cm tall, yellow to reddish, lacking chlorophyll, growing as a saprophyte on decaying plant remains. Stem covered with scale-like leaves. Flowers solitary or in terminally drooping spike, becoming erect again in fruit. Inside of corolla, stamens and style hairy. Calyx and corolla fall off after flowering. Fruit taller than wide.

Flowering season: Jun-Aug

Habitat: Woodland, dunes

Distribution: Most of Europe; Asia; N America.

2

Primrose* ❀ ☒ *Primula vulgaris*

(Primrose Family)

Compact plant, growing to 15cm tall. Leaves in a rosette, to 15cm long, gradually tapering towards base, pale green and hairless above, grey-green and hairy below, with finely toothed margin (margins rolled under when young). Flowers on long stalks, to 3cm across. Calyx to 15mm long, with sharp edges. Corolla lobes opening into broad, flat face. Fruit a 5-10mm long capsule.

Flowering season: Feb-May

Habitat: Open deciduous woods, scrub, grassland

Distribution: Much of Europe, especially W and S; Caucasus; Turkey; N Africa

Note: In S Europe there are plants with different flower colour: white in W Mediterranean, pink or red in Balkans. Elsewhere non-yellow Primroses are usually of garden origin.

3

Cowslip* ❀ ☒ *Primula veris*

(Primrose Family)

To 30cm tall, softly hairy. Leaves basal, wrinkled, long, ovate, dark green above, pale green beneath, irregularly notched margin. Flowers scented, clustered on a long, leafless stem. Calyx teeth ovate. Corolla to 15mm across, tube-shaped at base, with cup-shaped opening, deep yellow, with orange markings in centre. Fruit a 5-10mm long, oval capsule.

Flowering season: Apr-May

Habitat: Dry grassland and scrub

Distribution: Most of Europe; Asia.

Similar species: Oxlip*☒, *P. elatior*, has paler, scentless flowers, lanceolate calyx teeth, wider corolla. Damp meadows and woods, and montane grassland in continental Europe. In Britain a rare flower of certain E Anglian woods.

1
2
3

1 Tufted Loosestrife* ☒ *Lysimachia thyrsiflora*

(Primrose Family)

To 60cm tall, with upright, mostly unbranched stems, sparsely hairy. Leaves opposite, the upper ones narrowly lanceolate, to 10cm long, unstalked, somewhat rolled at the margins, with red spots and sparsely hairy. Flowers in dense, stalked inflorescences, about 1-3cm long, in the axils of middle stem leaves. 5-7 sepals, 2.5-4.5mm long, narrowly lanceolate, hairless. Petals 5-7, 3-6mm long, linear, spotted with red towards tip. Capsule about 3mm long, with red spots.

Flowering season: May-Jul

Habitat: Banks, ditches, wet meadows

Distribution: N Europe, from Alps northwards; Siberia; N America. Rare in Britain (N England and S Scotland).

2 Creeping Jenny* ✿ *Lysimachia nummularia*

(Primrose Family)

To 5cm, hairless, plant with creeping stems, up to 50cm long, freely rooting. Leaves opposite, round to ovate, stalked, often with heart-shaped base, sometimes spotted with red. Flowers solitary, in the axils of middle leaves. Flower stalks about as long as leaves. Sepals 5, 7-10mm long, narrowly heart-shaped, with red spots; petals 5, Sep-16mm long, ovate, with red spots.

Flowering season: May-Jul

Habitat: Damp meadows, gardens, ditches, wet woods, woodland edges

Distribution: Most of Europe; spread to many parts of the world. In Britain, absent from C and N Scotland. In Ireland, mainly in N.

Similar species: Yellow Pimpernel*, *L. nemorum*, has upright stem, oval leaves with translucent spots, flowers in axils of upper leaves, sepals linear, petals lanceolate, unspotted. Yellow flowers with 5 petal-lobes are star-shaped and up to 1.2cm across. Darker yellow spot at the centre of each flower. In damp woods and scrub.

3 Yellow Loosestrife* *Lysimachia vulgaris*

(Primrose Family)

Hairy plant, to 1.5m tall. Leaves opposite or in whorls of 3-4, lanceolate, to 15cm long, short-stalked or stalkless, red spotted, and thickly hairy beneath. Inflorescence a panicle, usually terminal. Usually 5 sepals, 3-5mm long, lanceolate, with glandular hairs and red-edged. Petals 7-12mm long, ovate, without red spots. Capsule 4-5mm long, unspotted.

Flowering season: Jun-Jul

Habitat: Wet woods, ditches, river banks, scrub, meadows, marsh

Distribution: Most of Europe; N Africa, E to Japan.

Similar species: Dotted Loosestrife*, *L. punctata*, is a garden plant which often escapes (native of S Europe). It has unspotted leaves in whorls of 3-6, thickly hairy on both sides, sepals without red-edges, and red-spotted petals.

1
2|3

1

Fringed Water-lily* ❀ ☒ *Nymphoides peltata*

(Bogbean Family)

Floating water plant with alternate leaves (opposite in flowering stems). Floating leaves round, with heart-shaped base, thick and leathery, stalked, light green above, red-violet below, dotted with wart-like glands. Flowers mostly in clusters, but not all flowering together, long-stalked, emerging just above the water surface. Calyx divided into 5, almost to base. Corolla 3-5cm across, with short, funnel-shaped tube and 5 spreading lobes, fringed at margins, hairy inside mouth. Fruit 1.5-2.5cm long, narrowly oval.

Flowering season: Jun-Aug

Habitat: Standing or slow-flowing, eutrophic water, warm in summer

Distribution: C and S Europe; E to Japan. In Britain mainly S England.

Note: When not in flower can be confused with the true water-lilies (see p. 36), but the warty underside of the leaves distinguishes this unrelated species. Also grown in garden ponds and introduced to ponds and lakes.

2

Wood Sage* *Teucrium scorodonia*

(Mint Family)

Erect, downy plant to 50cm tall, with rectangular stem, usually branched only towards the top. Leaves stalked, to 7cm long, ovate, heart-shaped at base, toothed and wrinkled. Flowers 9-12mm long, short-stalked, solitary or in pairs in the axils of small bracts. Flowers all tend to bend over to same side of inflorescence. Calyx tubular or bell-shaped, curved and 2-lipped, the upper lip broad, oval and much larger. Corolla pale yellow to greenish-yellow, with projecting tube and down-curved lower lip.

Flowering season: Jun-Oct

Habitat: Open woods, heaths, scrub, wood margins

Distribution: Most of Europe, except N and E. Rare in C Ireland.

Note: All Germander (*Teucrium*) species are readily identified by their characteristic corolla shape. This lacks apparent upper lip, since this is divided and the two halves deflected to the sides, giving the lower lip a 5-lobed appearance (see also p. 134, Wall Germander).

1
2

1

Yellow Archangel* *Lamiastrum galeobdolon*

(Mint Family)

To 60cm tall plant with erect hairy stem, producing runners during or shortly after flowering. Leaves stalked, broadly lanceolate, coarsely toothed. Flowers in unstalked whorled clusters in the axils of upper pairs of stem leaves. Corolla yellow, 1.7-2.5cm long; lower lip flecked brown, 3-lobed; calyx with long, pointed teeth; anthers yellow.

Flowering season: Apr-Aug

Habitat: Mixed deciduous woods, scrub, tall-herb communities

Distribution: Most of Europe, N to S Scandinavia. Absent from much of Ireland and Scotland.

2

Yellow Woundwort *Stachys recta*

(Mint Family)

Somewhat hairy plant with rectangular stem, to 50cm tall. Leaves opposite, oblong, short-stalked, entire or shallowly toothed. Flowers unstalked, in whorled clusters in axils of bracts. Corolla yellow, 1-2cm long, lips with turned back edges. Upper lip erect, lower lip 3-lobed, with brown spots.

Flowering season: Jun-Sep

Habitat: Rocks, meadows, edges of woods, scrub

Distribution: Most of Europe, but only reaching Britain as a rare alien.

3

Large-flowered Hemp-nettle*

(Mint Family) *Galeopsis speciosa*

To 1m tall, stiffly hairy plant with rectangular stem. Leaves stalked, ovate to lanceolate, rounded or wedge-shaped at base, and regularly toothed. Flowers in whorls in the axils of bracts. Corolla yellow, 1.5-2.5cm long; lower lip rectangular, usually violet.

Flowering season: Jul-Sep

Habitat: Woods, clearings, scrub, hedgerows, footpaths, as weed in crops

Distribution: Mainly C and E Europe; local in British Isles.

4

Sticky Sage ❁ ☒ *Salvia glutinosa*

(Mint Family)

To 1m tall, with sticky, rectangular stem. Leaves stalked, ovate, with heart-shaped base and serrated margin. Flowers in clusters of 2-6, in axils of small bracts. Corolla yellow, to 4cm long; upper lip sickle-shaped; lower lip with red-brown spots and stripes, 3-lobed.

Flowering season: Jul-Sep

Habitat: Mountain woods, tall-herb communities, scrub

Distribution: Mountains of C and S Europe; E to Himalaya. Absent from British Isles.

1
2|3
4

1 Dark Mullein* *Verbascum nigrum*

(Figwort Family)

To 1.2m tall, slightly hairy plant with several unbranched stems. Basal leaves ovate, with heart-shaped base, stalked. Stem leaves rounded, stalkless, hairless above. Flowers in groups of 2-4, making up dense spike. Corolla 15-20mm across, 5-lobed, pale yellow, deep red spots at base. Stamens with purple hairs on filaments.

Flowering season: Jun-Sep

Habitat: Dry grassland, weedy places, river banks

Distribution: Most of Europe, N to S Scandinavia; E to Siberia. In Britain mainly in S and E.

2 Great Mullein* *Verbascum thapsus*

(Figwort Family)

To 1.8m, covered in white, woolly hairs. Leaves long, elliptic, stem leaves winged along stem down to next leaf, lower leaves stalked. Flowers on short stalks, grouped together in a dense spike. Corolla pale yellow, with 5 lobes, open funnel-shaped, 18-22mm across. 2 longer stamen filaments with white, woolly hairs, 3-4 times as long as their anthers.

Flowering season: Jul-Sep

Habitat: Weedy places, woodland margins, clearings

Distribution: Most of Europe; N Asia.

Similar species: Orange Mullein, *V. phlomoides*. Upper leaves not running far down stem and flowers larger and flatter (30-35mm across). Stamen filaments 0.5-2 times as long as their anthers. Similar habitats. Casual only in Britain.

3 Common Toadflax* *Linaria vulgaris*

(Figwort Family)

Many-stemmed, hairless plant, to 90cm tall. Leaves lanceolate to linear, pointed, rather blue-green. Flowers short-stalked, in a dense spike. Calyx with 5 pointed lobes. Corolla pale yellow, 16-30mm long, 2-lipped, the upper lip with an orange palate closing entrance, and an obvious, pointed spur at base.

Flowering season: Jun-Oct

Habitat: Dry grassland, footpaths, waste ground

Distribution: Most of Europe; W Asia.

1
2|3

1

Large Yellow Foxglove ☠ ❀ ☒

(Figwort Family) *Digitalis grandiflora*

Hairy plant, to 1m tall. Leaves unstalked, long-ovate, toothed. Flowers short-stalked, nodding. Flower stalks and the 5-partite calyx with glandular hairs. Corolla yellow with brown veins, 3-4.5cm long, bell-shaped, inflated, with weakly developed lip.
Flowering season: Jun-Jul. *Habitat:* Woodland edges, scrub, tall-herb communities
Distribution: C, S and E Europe; E to Siberia.
Similar species: Small Yellow Foxglove, *D. lutea*, occurs in similar habitats, usually on calcareous soils. It is mainly hairless, corolla 20-25mm long, with pointed, 2-lobed upper lip. Both yellow foxgloves appear as garden escapes only in British Isles.

2

Yellow-rattle* *Rhinanthus minor*

(Figwort Family)

Almost hairless plant to 50cm tall. Leaves unstalked, lanceolate, toothed. Bracts narrow, triangular, with toothed margins, lower teeth to 8mm long. Corolla 15-20mm long, with straight tube. Calyx inflated when fruiting. Upper lip with 2 short, bluish teeth; lower lip decurved.
Flowering season: Jun-Sep. *Habitat:* Grassland of all types, semi-parasite on grasses
Distribution: Throughout region.
Note: This genus is a difficult one. Several similar species occur in Europe; one of the commoner on mainland Europe is the Greater Yellow-rattle*, *R. angustifolius*. It has yellow-green bracts and up-curved corolla tube. Very rare in Britain. The photo is of a form of Greater Yellow-rattle.

3

Common Cow-wheat* *Melampyrum pratense*

(Figwort Family)

To 30cm tall, somewhat hairy plant with opposite, lanceolate leaves. Flowers in a raceme. Bracts lanceolate, with few teeth. Calyx 5-lobed, 5-7mm long. Corolla pale yellow, long, tube-shaped, 10-16mm long, 2-lipped, with closed throat.
Flowering season: Jun-Aug. *Habitat:* Meadows, heaths, scrub, woods: a semi-parasite of herbs and grasses. *Distribution:* Most of Europe; E to W Siberia.

4

Moor-king ❀ ☒ *Pedicularis sceptrum-carolinum*

(Figwort Family)

Hairless, to 1m tall. Leaves pinnate with long, toothed lobes. Calyx teeth long, toothed. Corolla fused with enclosed throat, yellow. Margin of lower lip blood-red.
Flowering season: Jun-Aug. *Habitat:* Fens, wet meadows
Distribution: N Europe, Alps. Not in Britain or Ireland.

5

Greater Bladderwort* ☒ *Utricularia vulgaris*

(Bladderwort Family)

Submerged stems 30-100cm long. Leaves pinnate and feathery, with many bladder-shaped structures which trap water insects. Flowers stalked, emerging above water surface. 2-lipped, throat closed by upwardly directed lower lip.
Flowering season: Jun-Aug. *Habitat:* Still water
Distribution: Most of Europe; Asia; N America.

1|2

3|4

5

1 Lady's Bedstraw*

Galium verum

(Bedstraw Family)

To 60cm tall, with rounded stem with 4 longitudinal ridges. Leaves in whorls of 8-12, narrowly linear and with pointed tips, rolled downwards at margins, about 1mm across, and with soft hairs below. Flowers small, numerous, thickly clustered in a much-branched terminal inflorescence. Calyx absent, corolla 4-lobed, smelling strongly of honey.

Flowering season: Jun-Sep

Habitat: Dry grassland, footpaths, open woods

Distribution: Most of Europe; N Asia.

FLOWER
Lady's Bedstraw

2 Goldenrod*

Solidago virgaurea

(Daisy Family)

Plant with erect stem, growing to 1m tall. Basal leaves elliptic, long-stalked and shiny. Stem leaves narrower, entire or toothed, narrowing towards winged stalk. Flower heads in terminal spikes. Bract scales narrow, lanceolate, with fleshy margins. Ray florets longer than involucre and golden yellow, like the tube florets. Fruit with pappus.

Flowering season: Jul-Oct

Habitat: Poor grassland, clearings

Distribution: Most of Europe; N Asia; N America.

3 Early Goldenrod* ❀

Solidago gigantea

(Daisy Family)

To 2m tall, with hairless lower stem. Leaves lanceolate, toothed, hairless below, or with short hairs along veins. Flower heads small, erect, in dense clusters on drooping stalks. Ray florets somewhat longer than involucre and tube florets. Fruit with pappus.

Flowering season: Aug-Oct

Habitat: Wet woodland, tall herb communities, footpaths

Distribution: N America; garden plant in Europe, including British Isles; widely naturalized.

Similar species: Canadian Goldenrod ❀, *S. canadensis*, has thickly hairy stem and undersides of leaves. Ray florets not longer than involucre and tube florets. Similar habitats. Introduced.

FLOWERHEAD
Canadian Goldenrod

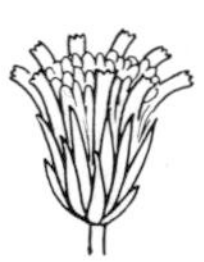

FLOWERHEAD
Early Goldenrod

1|2
3

1

Prickly Lettuce* *Lactuca serriola*

(Daisy Family)

Erect, branched plant growing to about 1.8m tall. Leaves are oblong, with small spines at the edges. Flower heads about 12mm across, arranged in a loose inflorescence.

Flowering season: Jul-Sep.*Habitat:* Waste ground, roadsides
Distribution: Much of Europe, except far N, Ireland and Scotland. In Britain mainly in SE England.

2

Wall Lettuce* *Mycelis muralis*

(Daisy Family)

Hairless plant to about 1m tall, with thin, erect stems. Leaves thin and usually deep reddish. Lower leaves pinnately lobed, upper ones less divided and clasping stem. Heads small, with regularly 5 spreading florets (appearing like a 5-petalled flower).

Flowering season: Jun-Sep. *Habitat:* Woods, old walls, rocks
Distribution: Much of Europe, except far N.

3

Common Fleabane* *Pulicaria dysenterica*

(Daisy Family)

Softly hairy plant growing to about 60cm tall, with underground runners and usually a much-branched stem. Leaves long, the lower ones stalked and dying off towards flowering time. Upper leaves heartshaped at the base and encircling stem. Flower heads 15-30mm across in umbel-like heads. Involucre with many narrow, pointed bracts. Ray florets narrow and spreading.

Flowering season: Jul-Sep. *Habitat:* Damp meadows, river banks
Distribution: Europe; North and West Asia; North Africa. Throughout Britain and Ireland, but not in N Scotland.

4

Nodding Bur-marigold* *Bidens cernua*

(Daisy Family)

Plant to 1.2m tall with opposite, lanceolate, toothed and almost unstalked leaves. Flower heads nodding when fully developed and with leaflike bracts. Both radiate and non-radiate variants occur (photograph shows the radiate one).

Flowering season: Aug-Oct. *Habitat:* Damp places, ponds and ditchsides
Distribution: Most of Europe; North Asia; North America. Throughout Britain and Ireland, but not in N Scotland.
Similar species: Trifid Bur-marigold°, *B. tripartita,* has stalked, 3-lobed leaves and is found in similar habitats.

5

Yellow Chamomile* *Anthemis tinctoria*

(Daisy Family)

Plant to 50cm tall with simple or twice pinnate, hairy leaves. Flower heads terminal. Involucral scales with dry borders. Long, pointed, translucent scales between tube florets.

Flowering season: Jun-Sep. *Habitat:* Dry slopes, scrub; mainly on calcareous soils.
Distribution: Warmer parts of Europe and North Asia. Introduced, rare and locally naturalized in Britain.

1|2
3
4|5

1

Tansy* *Tanacetum vulgare*

(Daisy Family)

Leafy, aromatic plant growing to 1.2m tall with a mostly hairless stem, branched towards the top. Leaves unstalked, pinnately lobed, with long, sharp-toothed leaflets. Inflorescence an umbellike head. Individual flower heads golden yellow and 6-10mm across. Involucre domed, with green bract scales arranged rather like roof tiles. Florets all tube-type, and extending well beyond bracts.

Flowering season: Jul-Sep

Habitat: Tall-herb communities, river banks, weedy areas, waste ground

Distribution: Most of Europe; West Asia. Throughout British Isles, but less common in Ireland and Scotland.

2

Colt's-foot* *Tussilago farfara*

(Daisy Family)

Plant to about 25cm tall. Flowering stems appearing before the leaves, unbranched and covered with thick white weblike hairs and with lanceolate, pointed pinkish scalelike leaves. Flower heads terminal, 30-40mm across. Involucre with a single row of scalelike bracts. Ray florets narrow and spreading, to 14mm long and bright yellow in colour. Leaves large, basal, long-stalked and rounded with a heartshaped base. Leaf margins toothed. Upper side of leaf weakly hairy, underside with a dense covering of white felty hairs.

Flowering season: Mar-Apr

Habitat: Banks, footpaths, damp fields, waste ground

Distribution: Most of Europe; N Asia; N Africa. Throughout British Isles.

Similar species: The genus *Petasites* is closely related. Members are easily distinguished by their whitish-pink flowering heads lacking ray florets. The leaves however are easier to confuse with those of Colt's-foot. They also appear after the flowers and both genera grow in similar habitats. Butterbur° *P. hybridus* (see p. 236); White Butterbur°, *P. albus*, has sparse whitish hairs on the underside of the leaves and the lobes at leaf base nearly meeting.

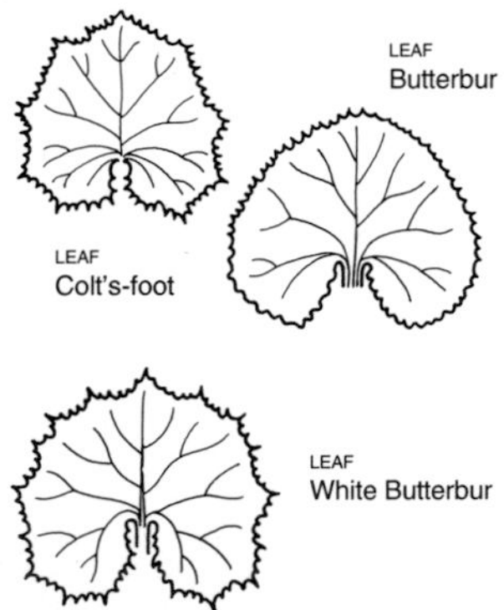

1
2

1

Oxford Ragwort* *Senecio squalidus*

(Daisy Family)

Branched, bushy plant, to about 40cm tall. Leaves pinnately lobed, the upper ones clasping stem, lower ones with winged stalk. Flower heads about 15-25mm across and bright yellow. Involucral bracts are tipped black.

Flowering season: Jun-Dec

Habitat: Old walls, waste ground, especially by railways

Distribution: S and C Europe, but widely naturalized. Throughout England and Wales; rare in Ireland and Scotland.

2

Groundsel* *Senecio vulgaris*

(Daisy Family)

Almost hairless or sparsely hairy annual plant growing to about 40cm tall with irregularly branched stem. Leaves divided, with short, toothed lobes. Lower leaves with short stalks, upper leaves encircling stem. Flower heads many, flower stalks lengthening when in fruit. Involucre cylindrical, 4-5mm across, bract scales in a single row 5-8mm long, hairless with black tips. Involucre also has 8-10 short black outer bract scales. Ray florets mainly absent (sometimes a few short ones present). Fruit hairy, with pappus.

Flowering season: Feb-Nov

Habitat: Waste ground, fields, gardens, footpaths, woodland clearings

Distribution: Most of Europe except the far North.

3

Common Ragwort* ☠ *Senecio jacobaea*

(Daisy Family)

Hairy to almost hairless plant growing to 1m tall. Stem branched towards top. Leaves pinnately lobed, with a divided auricle encircling stem at the base. Inflorescence umbellike. Involucre with one row of scales and 12 very short scales at the base. Achene with pappus, outer ones hairless, those of disk (inner) hairy.

Flowering season: Jul-Sep

Habitat: Meadows, dry grassland, tall-herb communities

Distribution: Europe; N Asia.

Similar species: Hoary Ragwort*, *S. erucifolius,* has undivided auricles at the base, an involucre with 4-6 short scales (half the length of other bracts), and all achenes hairy.

4

Marsh Ragwort* ☠ *Senecio aquaticus*

(Daisy Family)

To about 80cm tall, with rather wide-angled branches and loose inflorescence. Lower leaves little-divided or entire. Flower heads 2.5-3cm across, with about 15-20 ray florets. Bracts not black-tipped. Achenes hairless.

*Flowering season:*Jul-Aug

Habitat: Marshes, ditches, wet meadows

Distribution: W Europe, N to S Scandinavia.

1
2|3
4

1

Viper's-grass* ☒ *Scorzonera humilis*

(Daisy Family)

Plant to 40cm tall. Leaves all basal, lanceolate to narrowly lanceolate, with entire margins, narrowing towards the base. Flower heads mostly solitary and terminal on a leafless stalk. Flowers only with ray florets. Involucral scales in many rows. Fruits with pappus.

Flowering season: May-Jun

Habitat: Boggy meadows and poor grassland.

Distribution: Europe, rarer towards the N and S. Very rare in England.

2

Smooth Sow-thistle* *Sonchus oleraceus*

(Daisy Family)

Plant to about 1m tall, branched towards the top. Leaves with rounded teeth or pinnately lobed, rarely entire. Flower heads long-stalked and consisting only of ray florets. Involucre hairless. Fruit with pappus. Stem leaves with pointed auricles at the base.

Flowering season: Jul-Oct

Habitat: Fields, weedy habitats

Distribution: most of Europe; Asia; N Africa.

Similar species: Prickly Sow-thistle°, *S. asper*, has rounded auricles on the stem leaves and the fruit has 3 longitudinal ridges. Perennial Sow-thistle°, *S. arvensis*, has large heads and involucres with yellow topped glandular hairs.

LEAF BASES
Smooth Sow-thistle Prickly Sow-thistle

3

Smooth Hawk's-beard* *Crepis capillaris*

(Daisy Family)

To 75cm tall, but often smaller. Wiry stems and many small yellow flower heads characterize this common, variable species. The fruits have conical heads.

Flowering season: Jun-Sep

Habitat: Grassland, heath, walls, roadsides, waste ground

Distribution: Throughout Europe, except far N.

4

Rough Hawk's-beard* *Crepis biennis*

(Daisy Family)

Hairy plant growing to lm tall. Leaves linear to lanceolate, deeply pinnately lobed. Lower leaves stalked, upper leaves stalkless. Flower heads stalked, to 3.5cm across, with only ray florets. Involucre 1.5cm across, inner bracts appressed, outer ones narrow. Involucre dark green, with stellate hairs and dark bristles. Fruits with pure white pappus.

Flowering season: May-Aug

Habitat: Meadows, waste ground

Distribution: most of Europe.

1|2

3

4

1

Goat's-beard*

Tragopogon pratensis

(Daisy Family)

Hairless plant growing to 60cm with few branches. Stem slightly thickened below flower head. Leaves narrowly lanceolate, pointed and entire, with enlarged base. Flower heads solitary or in small groups and with only ray florets. Involucre 25-35mm long, with 8 linear, pointed scales. Anthers yellow with black stripes. Fruits long-stalked, with feathery pappus. The plant illustrated is the large-flowered subsp. *orientalis*, a rare casual in the British Isles. Subsp. *pratensis* with ray florets more or less equalling involucral bracts, and subsp. *minor* with ray florets shorter than involucral bracts, both occur in the British Isles, but subsp. *minor* is much the commoner.

Flowering season: May-Jul

Habitat: Rich meadows, dry grassland, footpaths

Distribution: Most of Europe.

Note on biology: Flowers of this species represent a kind of biological clock. In good weather subsp. *orientalis* opens at around 11 o'clock, subsp. *pratensis* from about 2 o'clock in the afternoon.

Similar species: T. dubius has stem below inflorescence very much thickened, and 8-12 bract scales. In dry grassland, mostly on chalk. Not in British Isles.

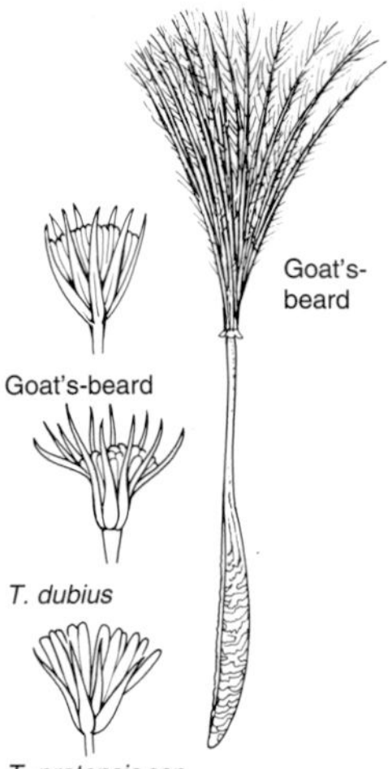

FLOWERHEADS AND FRUITS

2

Dandelion*

Taraxacum officinale

(Daisy Family)

Hairless or sparsely hairy plant to about 50cm tall. Leaves in a basal rosette with very uneven teeth, rarely entire. Flower heads solitary on a long leafless stem. Flowers with ray florets only. Involucre of small spreading scales on the outside and longer appressed narrow scales on the inside. Fruit with a long beak and umbrella-shaped feathery pappus.

Flowering season: Apr-Jun (-Dec)

Habitat: Rich meadows, pastures, fields, waste ground

Distribution: Found throughout Europe and W Asia in a wide range of subspecies.

Note: Like many of the composites whose flowers consist only of ray florets, this species has a white, milky juice containing latex.

Dandelion

1
2

1

Mouse-ear Hawkweed* *Hieracium pilosella*

(Daisy Family)

Plant to about 30cm tall with single flower heads on leafless stalks. Leaves in basal rosettes, with bristles on the upper surface and margins and white, felty hairs below. Rosette sends out leafy runners which can root at the tips. Involucre glandular and hairy. Flowers with ray florets only. Fruit with pappus.

Flowering season: May-Oct

Habitat: Dry grassland, heaths

Distribution: Most of Europe; N Asia; N America.

2

Nipplewort* *Lapsana communis*

(Daisy Family)

Plant to 1m tall. Stem with bristly hairs towards the base, hairless and branched higher up. Basal leaves pinnately lobed, with large oval terminal lobe. Upper leaves lanceolate, toothed and stalkless. Flower heads small, 10-20mm across, with pale yellow ray florets. Fruits without pappus.

Flowering season: Jun-Aug

Habitat: Deciduous woods, scrub, gardens, footpaths

Distribution: Most of Europe; W Asia; N Africa.

3

Few-leaved Hawkweed*

(Daisy Family) *Hieracium murorum* group

Plant to 60cm tall with a stem branched only towards the top, and with few leaves. Basal leaves ovate, toothed lower down and heartshaped and hairy at the base. Stem leaves smaller, few in number, usually 1 or 2. Flower heads few and with ray florets only. Involucre glandular, hairless. Fruit with pappus.

Flowering season: May-Jul

Habitat: Deciduous woods, scrub, mountain meadows, walls

Distribution: Most of Europe; N Asia.

4

Umbellate Hawkweed*

(Daisy Family) *Hieracium umbellatum* group

Softly hairy plant to about 80cm tall, with leafy stems and no basal rosette. Leaves narrowly lanceolate, with curved-back margins. Flower heads in a flat-topped inflorescence. Involucral bracts virtually hairless and curved back. Fruit with pappus.

Flowering season: Jun-Oct. *Habitat:* Woods, roadsides, heaths; on dry soils

Distribution: Throughout most of Europe.

5

Leafy Hawkweed* *Hieracium sabaudum* group

(Daisy Family)

The hawkweeds in this group tend to grow tall and rather bushy. They have leafy stems and broad, often oval leaves. The leaf edges do not curve back.

Flowering season: Jun-Oct. *Habitat:* woods, roadsides, hedges

Distribution: Throughout most of Europe.

Note: The genus *Hieracium*, like *Taraxacum*, consists of very many microspecies, reproducing by apomixis (a form of asexual reproduction). Three common European groups are illustrated here.

1

2|3

4|5

1

(Snake's-head) Fritillary* ❀ ☒

(Lily Family) *Fritillaria meleagris*

Hairless plant to 40cm tall. Leaves few and alternate, linear, bluish green in colour. Flowers solitary or in twos, drooping and bell-shaped, to 3.5cm long. Perianth segments ovate with a checkerboard pattern of purplish-red and pale areas (more rarely pure white).

Flowering season: Apr-May

Habitat: Damp meadows

Distribution: W Europe and local in C and S Europe. Local in England and Wales (possibly introduced).

Note: This species has disappeared from many of its earlier habitats and is amongst the most threatened plants in many parts of Europe. It has recently been introduced via the garden trade to several places. However the plants that have been re-introduced in this way are nearly always genetically different from the original wild stock.

2

Martagon Lily* ❀ ☒ *Lilium martagon*

(Lily Family)

Robust plant growing to 1m tall. Lower leaves alternate, upper leaves in whorls and elliptic to lanceolate. Flowers stalked and nodding, in loose terminal racemes. Perianth segments 6, long and curved backwards, pale brownish-red in colour with darker spots. Anthers long-stalked, dark red.

Flowering season: Jun-Jul

Habitat: Mountain pastures and mountain woods, particularly on calcareous soils.

Distribution: Most of Europe; Temperate Asia. Possibly native in parts of England, but often introduced via gardens.

Similar species: L. bulbiferum has alternate, linear leaves sometimes with brown bulbils in the axils. Flowers solitary or in groups, 4-6cm long, with upright pale red or yellowish-red bracts. *Flowering season:* May-Jul. *Habitat:* Warm slopes, woodland margins and hedges in mountainous parts of C Europe and the Alps.

Note on Biology: Many members of the lily family overwinter or withstand an extended dry period by means of bulbs or bulbils. As soon as conditions are suitable they sprout and come into flower very quickly. Many early-flowering species are plants of this type. By developing lateral bulbs and bulbils they are able to propagate themselves vegetatively. Many species of *Allium* also develop vegetative bulbils between the flowers in the inflorescence.

1
2

1

Meadow Saffron (Autumn Crocus)*☠❀

(Lily Family) *Colchicum autumnale*

Hairless plant to 25cm tall. Leaves all basal, linear-lanceolate and entire, with many parallel veins, appearing with oval or linear capsule in spring. Flowers in 1s to 3s, opening in the Autumn. Flower a long reddish-purple tube with 6 long corolla lobes. 6 stamens and 3 styles, extending well clear of the corolla tube.

Flowering season: Aug-Sep

Habitat: Damp meadows

Distribution: Most of Europe.

2

Chives*❀

Allium schoenoprasum

(Lily Family)

Hairless plant to 50cm tall with a hollow stem bearing leaves very high up. Leaves tubular, surrounding stem with a sheath. Flowers in a terminal rounded cluster, protected by 2 ovate bracts. Perianth segments 6, lanceolate and pointed, 7-15mm long, longer than stamens.

Flowering season: Jun-Aug

Habitat: Damp meadows, river banks, flushes

Distribution: Most of Europe, especially on high ground; much of Asia; N America. Widely cultivated as a culinary herb.

3

Keeled Garlic*

Allium carinatum

(Lily Family)

Hairless plant to 60cm tall. Leaves on lower half of stem, grasslike and flat, surrounding stem with a sheathlike base. Flowers in a rounded umbellike inflorescence which also contains bulbils. Inflorescence protected by 2 long linear bracts. Flowers long-stalked. Perianth segments 6, 4-7mm long and only half as long as stamens.

Flowering season: Jun-Jul

Habitat: Dry grassland

Distribution: C Europe; Italy; Balkans. Naturalized and very local in British Isles.

Similar species: Field Garlic°, *Allium oleraceum*. Leaves grooved, perianth segments as long as stamens. Similar habitats.

4

Round-headed Leek*☒ *Allium sphaerocephalum*

(Lily Family)

Hairless plant to 60cm tall. Stem with leaves beyond midpoint. Leaves deeply grooved above and sheathing stem at base. Flowers in a dense rounded umbellike inflorescence with two small oval pointed bracts. Perianth segments 4-5mm long, shorter than stamens.

Flowering season: Jun-Jul

Habitat: Rocks, dry grassland, mostly on calcareous soils.

Distribution: C and SE Europe, east to Turkey. In Britain rare (Avon Gorge); also in Channel Islands.

1

2|3

4

1

Marsh Gladiolus ☒ *Gladiolus palustris*

(Iris Family)

Hairless plant to 50cm tall. Leaves laterally compressed, long and pointed and with distinct longitudinal veins. Flowers in groups of 3-6, nodding over to one side at the end of stem. Perianth segments reddish-purple, oval, somewhat pointed. 3 stamens.
Flowering season: Jun-Jul. *Habitat:* Damp meadows
Distribution: C Europe; Italy; Balkans.
Similar species: Wild Gladiolus*☒, *G. illyricus* is a rare and local plant of heathy scrub and woodland. It is found from S England (New Forest only) and W France southwards.

2

Lax-flowered Orchid* ☒ *Orchis laxiflora*

(Orchid Family)

To 1m tall, with unspotted leaves. Flowers reddish-purple. Central lobe of lip short or absent. Spur shorter than ovary. Bracts with 3-7 veins.
Flowering season: Apr-Jun. *Habitat:* marshes and damp meadows
Distribution: Scattered N to S Sweden. In British Isles only in Channel Islands.
Similar species: Early-purple Orchid*, *O. mascula* (p. 98) but taller, with unspotted leaves.

3

Military Orchid* ☒ *Orchis militaris*

(Orchid Family)

Hairless plant to 50cm tall, lower leaves elliptic and pointed, upper leaves smaller, entire. Flowers in a dense spike. 6 perianth segments, the upper 5 pale pink and projecting forwards into a hood, the lower one 5-lobed, pinkish-purple, with white spots on the lower lip.
Flowering season: May-Jun . *Habitat:* Fen meadows, moist grassland; on calcareous soils.
Distribution: C and S Europe; Caucasus; Siberia. North to S Sweden and in a few protected sites in S E England.

4

Lady Orchid* ☒ *Orchis purpurea*

(Orchid Family)

Hairless plant growing to 70cm tall. Leaves broadly elliptic and pointed, clustered together at the base of the stem. 6 perianth segments, the upper 5 oval-shaped with a purple hood, the lower one 4-lipped pale pink.
Flowering season: May-Jun. *Habitat:* Woods, scrub, dry grassland
Distribution: C and S Europe; Turkey. Just gets into the British flora as a rare species in Kent.

5

Heath Spotted-orchid* ☒ *Dactylorhiza maculata*

(Orchid Family)

Hairless plant to 60cm tall. Lower leaves oval with dark spots, upper leaves smaller and narrower. 6 perianth segments pale lilac in colour, the upper 5 not forming a hood and projecting forwards together. Lower lip 3-lobed.
Flowering season: May-Aug. *Habitat:* Marshy meadows
Distribution: Most of Europe; N Asia. Locally common throughout British Isles, but rare in E England.

1|2
3
4|5

1

Green-winged Orchid* ☒ *Orchis morio*

(Orchid Family)

Hairless plant growing to 40cm tall. Lower leaves linear-elliptic and pointed. Middle and upper leaves sheathlike. Flowers in a loose spike, purple or pink, more rarely whitish. 6 perianth segments, the upper 5 fused to form a short hood and with green veins. Lower perianth segments forming a shallowly-lobed lip, with a spur behind.

Flowering season: Apr-Jun

Habitat: Grassland

Distribution: Most of Europe; Caucasus. Mainly in the S of Britain and Ireland, local. Only in the extreme S of Scandinavia.

2

Broad-leaved Marsh-orchid* ☒

(Orchid Family) *Dactylorhiza majalis*

Hairless plant growing to 60cm tall, with long oval to lanceolate leaves, pointed at the tip and mostly with dark spots. Inflorescence a dense, many-flowered spike. Perianth segments 6, purple, the upper 5 segments erect, the lower one forming a weakly-lobed lip, broader than long and with a spur at the base.

Flowering season: May-Jun

Habitat: damp meadows, ditches, flush communities

Distribution: C and S Europe; Turkey; Siberia. Found also in the W of Ireland and a few places in N W Scotland and Wales.

Note: The marsh-orchids are a difficult group to identify; the species are variable and intermediates occur. The commonest British member of this group is the Southern Marsh-orchid*, *D. praetermissa,* which has dark pinkish-purple flowers and often unspotted leaves.

Early Marsh-orchid*, *D. incarnata,* has narrower, unspotted leaves and usually paler pink flowers.

3

Early-purple Orchid* ☒ *Orchis mascula*

(Orchid Family)

Hairless plant to 50cm tall with lanceolate basal leaves and sheathlike upper leaves. Inflorescence a loose spike. 6 perianth segments, purple in colour. Upper 3 lanceolate, erect and pointed, 2 of others broader and recurved. Lowest segment a deeply 3-lobed lip with a long spur behind.

Flowering season: May-Jun

Habitat: Mountain pastures, dry grassland, open deciduous woods

Distribution: W, C and S Europe; Turkey.

Note: The leaves of this species are usually glossy green, with dark purple blotches. However, forms with unblotched leaves (as in the photograph) also occur.

Note on Biology: Coevolution with insect pollinators has produced perhaps the greatest variety of flower shapes of any plant family. Such specialisations include many different kinds of lip shape and colour, evolved to mimic aspects of the females of certain insects, including flies and bees. Male insects pollinate the flowers as they attempt to mate with the fake females. The anthers carry pollinia, which are masses of pollen grains, all stuck together.

1
2|3

1

Fragrant Orchid* ☒ *Gymnadenia conopsea*

(Orchid Family)

Hairless plant growing to 60cm tall with lanceolate leaves up to 15cm long. Upper leaves smaller. Bracts about as long as ovaries. Flowers smell very strongly of carnations or cloves. Outer perianth segments 5-6mm long, the inner, upper ones smaller and rounded. Lip evenly 3-lobed with slightly longer central lobe. Spur thin, up to 1.5 to 2 times as long as ovary.

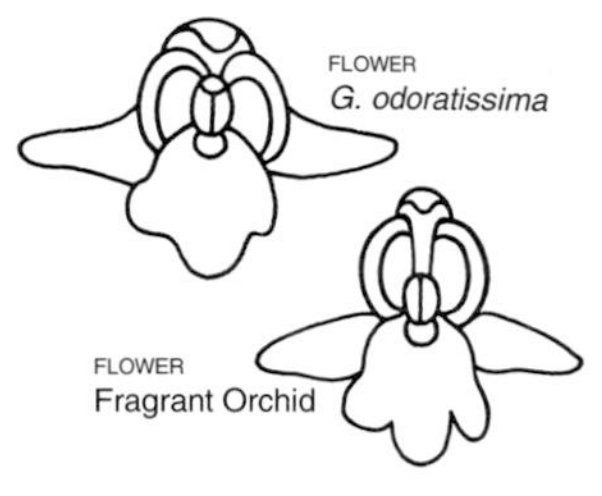

Flowering season: May-Aug
Habitat: Dry grassland, rocky slopes, open woodland; on calcareous soils
Distribution: Europe; N Asia.
Similar species: G. odoratissima has a spur about as long as the ovary, and a longer central lobe to the lip. Not found in British Isles.

2

Burnt Orchid* ☒ *Orchis ustulata*

(Orchid Family)

Hairless plant to about 30cm tall. Leaves lanceolate and unspotted, narrowing towards the tip. Inflorescence at first cone-shaped, later cylindrical. Upper part of inflorescence (where the flowers have not yet opened) is a deep, dark brown colour giving the characteristic burnt appearance. Other flowers pale violet and scented. Outer and inner side perianth segments fused into a rounded hood. Lip 3-lobed, whitish, with dark red spots. Central lobe widening towards the tip and divided into 2. Spur cone-shaped, 1-1.5mm long, curved downwards.
Flowering season: May-Jul
Habitat: Dry grassland, on chalk and silicious soils
Distribution: S and C Europe; North to S Sweden; Caucasus. In Britain found scattered in England, and declining.

3

Red Helleborine* ☒ *Cephalanthera rubra*

(Orchid Family)

Plant to 50cm tall. Leaves oval to lanceolate, 6-12cm long. Upper part of stem with a dense covering of short, glandular hairs. Inflorescence open, 4 to 12-flowered. Bracts as long as or longer than ovaries. Outer and 2 upper inner perianth segments 15-20mm long and pointed, held close together in a bell-like shape. Lip usually concealed, undivided and shorter than the other perianth segments, and with a deep division between the lower and upper halves. No spur.
Flowering season: Jun-Jul
Habitat: Dry deciduous and pine woods on calcareous soils
Distribution: Europe, except the far N; W Asia. In Britain a very rare species with just a handful of localities in S England.

1|2
3

1

Common Bistort* ❀ *Polygonum bistorta*

(Dock Family)

A hairless plant growing to 80cm tall, with an upright unbranched stem and widely separated leaves. Leaves ovate with heartshaped base; to 20cm long. Lower leaves with winged stalks, the upper ones stalkless, all with a stem-enveloping stipule at the base. Inflorescence a dense terminal cylindrical spike. Flowers 5-lobed, pink to red in colour and 4-5mm long. Fruit a 4-5mm dark brown shiny triangular nut.

Flowering season: May-Jul

Habitat: Damp meadows, tall-herb communities, older scrub

Distribution: W and C Europe, S Europe only in mountains; N Asia; N America. Rare in Ireland. In Britain commonest in NW England.

Note: The Latin species name *bistorta* (meaning twice-twisted) refers to the shape of the rootstock. This species was quoted in 16th Century Herbals as Snakeroot, and extracts from the roots were used to treat snake bites. Previously the rootstock was held by apothecaries under the name of "Radix Bistortae". It is used as an internal medicine to treat diarrhoea, and externally for infections of the mouth and throat.

2

Amphibious Bistort* *Polygonum amphibium*

(Dock Family)

In water, a hairless plant with floating leaves and stems to 3m long, but there is also a land form (usually on damp mud) which has shorter stems and smaller, often hairy leaves. Leaves long and lanceolate to 20cm and long-stalked. Inflorescence a dense terminal spike. Perianth pink, not divided into calyx and corolla. Bracts 4 or 5 and about 5mm long. Seldom develops fruit.

Flowering season: Jun-Sep

Habitat: Ponds, ditches, standing water

Distribution: worldwide.

Similar species: Redshank°, *P. persicaria,* has fringed stipules and pink to red flowers 2.5-3mm long.

Pale Persicaria, *P. lapathifolium,* is similar, but the stipules are usually unfringed and flowers pink or white. Both are found on cultivated ground, waste places or muddy banks.

Note: Species of the genus *Potamogeton* (see p. 210) also have floating leaves. However they have greenish inflorescenses and much reduced individual flowers.

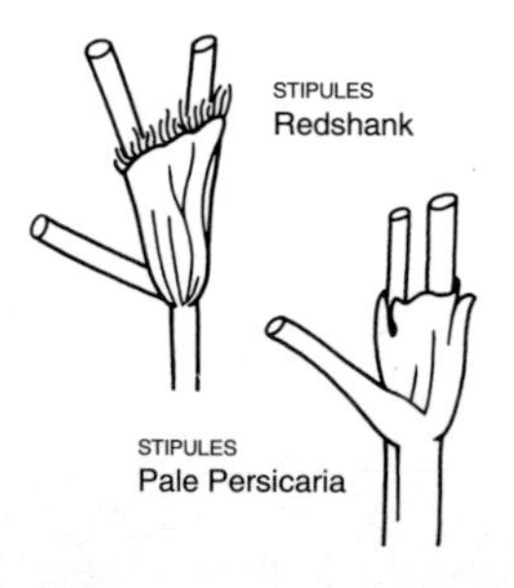

1
2

1

Soapwort*

Saponaria officinalis

(Pink Family)

Mainly hairy plant growing to 70cm tall. Leaves lanceolate and opposite, 3-veined, stalkless. Flowers weakly-scented and clustered in the axils of the upper leaves, often "doubled". Calyx tube-shaped, 17-25cm long, with 5 teeth. Petals 30-40mm, pale pink or white. Capsule one-celled and opening with 4 or 5 teeth. Seeds blackish, round or kidney-shaped, 1.8mm long.

Flowering season: Jun-Sep

Habitat: Footpaths, waste ground, river banks

Distribution: Europe; W Asia. Scattered through British Isles, often near old gardens (an anciently cultivated herb).

2

Ragged Robin*

Lychnis flos-cuculi

(Pink Family)

Hairless plant growing to 90cm tall. Both the flowering and nonflowering stems branched. Leaves narrow and opposite. Flowers arranged in panicle. Calyx 6-9mm long and 5-toothed. Petals pinkish red, 15-25mm long, deeply divided and with narrow tips. Capsule ovoid, narrowing towards the top, with 5 short teeth when open. Seeds rather prickly, 0.5-0.7mm broad.

Flowering season: May-Aug

Habitat: Fens, damp grassland, wet woodland

Distribution: Throughout Europe, but local in arable areas.

3

Red Soapwort ❀

Saponaria ocymoides

(Pink Family)

Low growing branched, creeping plant. Leaves obovate to narrowly spoon-shaped, opposite, to 3cm long. Flowers in clusters at the end of the stems. Calyx tubular, 7-12mm long, with glandular hairs and five teeth. Petals 12-18mm long, pale purplish red. Capsule oval, opening with 4 teeth. Seed kidney-shaped.

Flowering season: Apr-Oct

Habitat: rocks, pine woods, mainly on calcareous soils

Distribution: C and S Europe. Much grown in gardens in Britain, sometimes escaping.

4

Sticky Catchfly* ❀ ☒

Lychnis viscaria

(Pink Family)

Hairless plant growing to 60cm tall. Stem black and sticky below leaf nodes. Leaves narrow and pointed. Flowers in a panicle. Calyx 11-13mm long with 5 short, oval teeth and tinged dullish red. Petals 18-22mm long, red or purplish-red. Capsule ovoid, stalked and 5-toothed, 5-celled in the lower part and l-celled in the upper part. Seeds kidney-shaped, warty, 0.5cm across.

Flowering season: May-Jul

Habitat: Dry grassland, open woods; only on basic soils

Distribution: Europe; W Asia. In Britain rare and local in Wales and Scotland.

1|2
3
4

1

Red Campion*

Silene dioica

(Pink Family)

Hairy plant to 90cm tall with somewhat branched stem. Leaves broadly lanceolate to oval, stalkless and opposite. Flowers arranged in a loose panicle. Calyx 10-13mm long, reddish. Petals 15-25mm long, deeply notched at tip, with a 2-lobed scale at throat.

Flowering season: Apr-Sep

Habitat: Wet woodland, rich meadows, tall-herb communities

Distribution: Most of Europe; W Asia; N Africa.

Note: This species (and also the White Campion, p 168) is dioecious (ie separate male and female plants). Male plants have only male flowers with stamens. Female plants only female flowers with ovary and 5 styles.

PETAL SCALE
Red Campion

2

Large Pink ☒

Dianthus superbus

(Pink Family)

Hairless plant growing to 60cm tall, branched towards the top. Leaves opposite, narrowly lanceolate, to 8cm long. Flowers in a loose inflorescence. Calyx tube-like with two pairs of short, oval, pointed scales at base. Petals lilac to pale purple, greenish towards throat. Flowers 30-50mm across with divided, feathery petals.

Flowering season: Jun-Sep

Habitat: Damp meadows and heaths

Distribution: Most of Europe; W Asia. Absent from British Isles, though grown in gardens.

3

Maiden Pink* ☒

Dianthus deltoides

(Pink Family)

Hairy plant growing to 30cm tall. Stem branched towards top. Leaves opposite, narrowly lanceolate. Flowers solitary in the axils. Calyx tube-shaped, 5-toothed, with 2 scales at the base. Flowers deep or pale pink, to 20mm in diameter with toothed, white-spotted petals.

Flowering season: Jun-Sep

Habitat: Dry grassland, open woods, heaths

Distribution: Europe; W Asia. In Britain local, in lowlands. Also in SE Ireland, where probably introduced.

4

Carthusian Pink

Dianthus carthusianorum

(Pink Family)

Hairless plant growing to 45cm tall, with flowering stems growing up from a rosette of leaves. Leaves opposite, very narrowly lanceolate. Flowers in a dense cluster of up to 30, at the end of flowering stems. Calyx 14-18mm long, epicalyx scales short and pointed. Petals toothed at the tip.

Flowering season: Jun-Aug

Habitat: Dry grassland, open woods, rocks

Distribution: Central Europe. Occasional in Britain, only as garden escape.

1

2

3|4

1 Great Meadow-rue ❀ *Thalictrum aquilegifolium*

(Buttercup Family)

Hairless plant branched towards the top and growing to 1.2m tall. Leaves stalked, pinnate. Leaflets rounded or oval coarsely toothed and blue-green. Inflorescence a much branched many flowered panicle. Petals small 4-6mm yellow-green. Stamens many lilac (rarely white) and overtopping petals. Ripe fruits long, 5-7mm, nutlike, stalked.

Flowering season: May-Jul

Habitat: Wet woodland, tall-herb communities

Distribution: Europe (except N and W); E Asia. In British Isles as garden plant only.

2 Summer Pheasant's-eye ❀ *Adonis aestivalis*

(Buttercup Family)

Hairless plant growing to 40cm tall with dense covering of unstalked feathery pinnate leaves about a millimetre broad at the tip. Flowers solitary and terminal, 1-3.5cm across. Sepals 5, green and hairless. Petals 5-8, rather long. Many stamens. Fruits (achenes) keeled on the upper side, mostly with 2 teeth and with a short, straight beak at the tip.

Flowering season: May-Jul

Habitat: Agricultural fields; mostly on calcareous soils

Distribution: S and C Europe; Asia. Not in British Isles.

Similar species: Large Pheasant's-eye, *A. flammea,* has stem softly hairy at base, hairy sepals, and fruits have an obvious tooth on the underside and a twisted beak.

Pheasant's-eye°, *A. annua,* is a similar species which occurs rarely as an arable weed in Southern England.

ACHENES
Summer Pheasant's-Eye

ACHENES
Large Pheasant's-Eye

3 Hollow-root ❀ *Corydalis cava*

(Fumitory Family)

Hairless, unbranched plant growing to 20cm tall. Stem usually with 2 leaves. Leaves stalked, divided and toothed. Flowers in a dense spike. Bracts oval and entire. Sepals small, 0.5mm long. Corolla 2-lipped, spur at the base of the flower curved downwards at the end and as long as the rest of the flower.

Flowering season: Mar-May

Habitat: Deciduous woods, parks

Distribution: Central Europe. In British Isles only a garden escape.

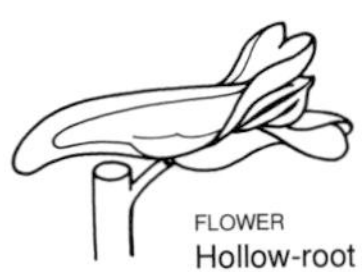

FLOWER
Hollow-root

1

2|3

1

Common Fumitory*

Fumaria officinalis

(Fumitory Family)

Hairless plant growing to 30cm tall. Stems weak, upright, branched, sometimes almost climbing. Leaves stalked, blue-green and feathery. Leaflets with deeply dissected lobes with tips three to four times as long as wide. Inflorescence with 10-15 flowers in the axils of the upper leaves. Bracts small, half to two-thirds as long as the fruitstalks. 2-toothed sepals on the sides of the flower about 1.5-2mm long. Corolla 6-9mm long, 2-lipped, with a rather short, thick spur. Fruit a stalked, rounded nut about 2-3mm in diameter, rather pinched in at the top.

Flowering season: Apr-Oct

Habitat: Arable fields, gardens, vineyards

Distribution: Europe; W Asia; N Africa.

Similar species: Few-flowered Fumitory*, *F. vaillantii*. Leaf tips 4-6 times as long as wide. Sepals 0.5-1mm long, pale pink. Fruit rounded, with a small point at the end. Fruitstalk scarcely longer than bract. Similar habitats. Very local in Britain.

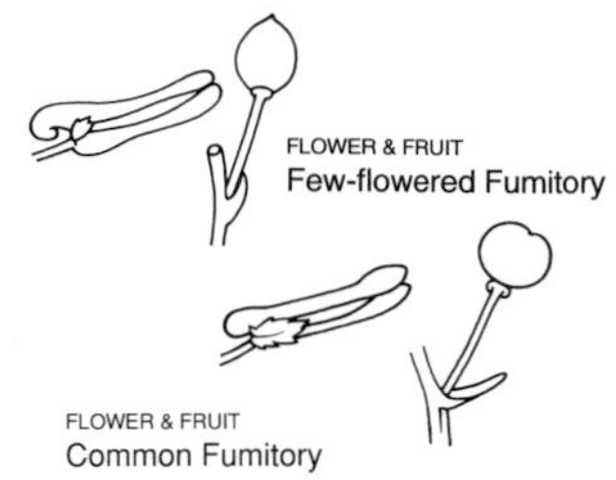

FLOWER & FRUIT
Few-flowered Fumitory

FLOWER & FRUIT
Common Fumitory

Note: There are several other species in Europe, but they are not at all easy to distinguish.

2

Common Poppy*

Papaver rhoeas

(Poppy Family)

Hairy plant to 70cm tall with feathery leaves and toothed leaflets. Flowers solitary and terminal, drooping in bud, becoming upright in flower. 2 sepals with bristly hairs. Sepals falling away during flowering. Petals 4, red, about 4cm long, often with black spots towards the base. Stamens numerous. Fruit a hairless rounded capsule with 8-18 spokeless ridges with many openings beneath.

Flowering season: May-Jul

Habitat: Arable fields, waste ground, edges of footpaths

Distribution: Virtually world-wide.

Similar species: Long-headed Poppy*, *P. dubium*. Petals 1-2cm long, fruit longer and narrower, with 6-9 ridges. Similar habitats. Rough Poppy*, *P. hybridum*, has a hairy fruit similar in shape to that of Common Poppy. Rarer, on clay and sandy soils. Prickly Poppy*, *P. argemone*, has a hairy, elongated fruit similar in shape to that of Long-headed Poppy. Found in crops and sandy soils.

CAPSULE
Common Poppy

CAPSULE
Long-headed Poppy

1
2

1

Five-leaved Coralroot ✿

(Cabbage Family) *Cardamine pentaphyllos*

Hairless plant growing to 60cm, with upright, branched stem. Lacks basal leaves at flowering time. Stem leaves alternate and stalked, with 5, starlike, toothed leaflets. Inflorescence nodding towards end of flowering period. Sepals 7-9mm long, hairless. Petals 15-25mm long, violet. Stamens shorter than corolla. Anthers yellow. Fruit a capsule, 4-7cm long and to about 5mm wide.

Flowering season: Apr-Jun

Habitat: Mixed deciduous woods, tall herb communities, streamsides

Distribution: Mountainous parts of S and C Europe. Not in British Isles.

2

Coralroot* ☒ *Cardamine bulbifera*

(Cabbage Family)

To about 60cm tall, hairy at base of stem, otherwise hairless. Stem erect and unbranched. No basal leaves at flowering time. Lower stem leaves pinnate, with 3-7 toothed leaflets, often arranged in a whorl. Upper stem leaves entire, toothed, with small bulbils in the axils. These bulbils later fall to the ground and grow into new plants. Sepals 6-7mm long, hairless. Petals 12-20mm long, violet, pink or whitish. Anthers yellow. Rarely fruiting.

Flowering season: May-Jun

Habitat: Deciduous woods, particularly beech woods

Distribution: Most of Europe; Turkey. In Britain rare, in S England only.

3

Cuckooflower, Lady's Smock*

(Cabbage Family) *Cardamine pratensis*

Almost hairless plant to 30cm tall, with a rosette of stalked, pinnate basal leaves each with 4-14 rounded leaflets. Terminal leaflet somewhat larger, to 1.5cm across. Stem leaves stalkless, with narrow, linear leaflets. Flowers 4-partite, to 1cm across. Sepals 3-4mm long. Petals 8-13mm long, pale pink or white. Fruit 2-4cm long, 1-1.5mm wide.

Flowering season: May-Jul

Habitat: Damp meadows, scrub, wet woodland

Distribution: Europe; Asia; N America.

Note: A very variable species, variously classified in European floras.

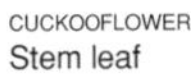

1

2|3

1

House-leek* ✿ ☒ *Sempervivum tectorum*

(Stonecrop Family)

Plant to 50cm tall with woolly glandular hairs, leafy stem and 2-5cm broad rosette. Rosette leaves bluish-green, with fringe of hairs (otherwise hairless), and reddish towards the tip. 12-16 petals, 9-11mm long, purple-red with darker stripes. Anthers purple.
Flowering season: Jun-Sep. *Habitat:* rocky outcrops, walls, roofs, dry grassland *Distribution:* Most of Europe. Introduced in Britain and widely planted on roofs and walls.

2

Great Burnet* *Sanguisorba officinalis*

(Rose Family)

Plant to 90cm tall with mostly leafless stem. Leaves pinnate, with roughly-toothed leaflets. Basal leaves in a rosette. Stem leaves alternate, smaller. Flowers brownish-red, small, lacking petals, in tight oval inflorescences.
Flowering season: Jun-Sep *Habitat:* meadows, ditches, footpath edges
Distribution: Most of Europe; eastwards to Japan. In Britain mainly C and N England. Absent from most of Scotland and rare in Ireland.
Similar species: Salad Burnet*, *S. minor,* is quite a common species of chalk and limestone grassland. It has pinnate basal leaves, reddish stems and dense, round flower heads.

3

Marsh Cinquefoil* *Potentilla palustris*

(Rose Family)

Plant to 30cm tall. Stem leaves pinnate, with 5-7 leaflets, dark green above, bluish-green and hairy below. Flowers in loose inflorescences, stalked, 5-partite, dark purple-red. Sepals petal-like, ovate. Petals much smaller. *Flowering season:* Jun-Aug. *Habitat:* Mires, bogs; avoids chalk *Distribution:* Almost all Europe; N Asia; N America. Locally common in N Britain and Ireland.

4

Red Clover* *Trifolium pratense*

(Pea Family)

To around 60cm. Leaf a large typical cloverleaf with three leaflets, often with pale white semicircular markings. The flower heads are rounded and pink, to 1.5cm long. Free part of stipule with a point to 3mm long. Fruit a pod opening near top.
Flowering season: May-Sep. *Habitat:* Grassy banks, roadsides, meadows
Distribution: Throughout.

5

Hare's-foot Clover* *Trifolium arvense*

(Pea Family)

Grey, hairy plant to 40cm tall. Leaves trifoliate. Inflorescence a long oval shape, 1-3cm, 1cm wide, stalked, with woolly hairs. Corolla 3-4mm long shorter than the calyx, at first white, later pink.
Flowering season: May-Aug
Habitat: Footpath edges, crop fields, open grassland; on acid soils
Distribution: Europe; spread almost worldwide. Locally common, and often coastal in Britain and Ireland. Absent from N Scotland.

1|2

3|4

5

1 Spiny Restharrow* *Ononis spinosa*

(Pea Family)

Plant to 50cm tall with 1 or 2 rows of hairs on stem, and usually with paired thorns in leaf axils. Lower leaves with 3 leaflets, upper leaves often entire. Flowers pink, short-stalked, usually solitary, in the axils of the upper stem leaves. Corolla 1-2.5cm long.

Flowering season: Jul-Oct

Habitat: Dry grassland, wasteland, footpath edges; mostly on calcareous soils

Distribution: C and W Europe northwards to S Scandinavia and Britain. Rare in Scotland: absent from Ireland.

Similar species: Common Restharrow°, *O. repens*, has stems hairy all round, and lacks spines.

2 Sainfoin* *Onobrychis viciifolia*

(Pea Family)

Plant to 60cm tall with upright hairy stems. Leaves 15cm long, pinnate. Leaflets elliptical, hairy below. Flowers pink to red; petals with darker veins, to about 15mm long.

Fruit semi-circular, to about 10mm, toothed at the edge.

Flowering season: May-Jul

Habitat: Meadows, footpaths, fields; calcareous soils

Distribution: Europe north to S Sweden. In England local, sometimes cultivated as a fodder crop.

FRUIT
Sainfoin

3 Crown Vetch* *Coronilla varia*

(Pea Family)

Virtually hairless plant to about 80cm tall with a low-lying stem. Often grows using other plants as a support. Leaves stalked, pinnate, with 11-25 leaflets. Leaflets oval with definite point at the end. Inflorescence a clustered spike. Flowers nodding in bud, becoming erect when open. Corolla 0.8-1.5cm long, pink to pale violet. Wings white, keel with dark violet tip. Fruit a slender, jointed pod 2-8cm long.

Flowering season: May-Oct

Habitat: Dry grassland, footpaths, scrub, wasteland; calcareous soils

Distribution: Most of Europe; Caucasus. Naturalized in British Isles.

4 Tufted Vetch* *Vicia cracca*

(Pea Family)

Plant to about 1.5m, with low-lying or clambering stems. Leaves pinnate, with 10-20 leaflets and terminal branched tendrils. Inflorescences blue-purple or pinkish-purple, long-stalked, many-flowered. Corolla 0.8-1.1cm long. Calyx teeth uneven, upper ones very short.

Flowering season: Jun-Sep

Habitat: Meadows, agricultural fields, scrub, woodland margins

Distribution: Europe; Asia.

1|2
3
4

1

Bush Vetch* *Vicia sepium*

(Pea Family)

Virtually hairless plant to about 50cm tall. Leaves pinnate, lowest without tendrils, all other leaves with branched tendrils. Leaflets broadly elliptical, hairy at the edge and on the undersides. Flowers in short-stalked clusters of up to 4, in the leaf axils. Corolla to 15mm long, dull violet. Calyx teeth unequal. Fruits to 4cm long, glossy black.
Flowering season: May-Jul
Habitat: Meadows, scrub, woodlands
Distribution: most of Europe; W and C Asia.

2

Common Vetch* *Vicia sativa*

(Pea Family)

Weakly hairy plant to about 50cm tall. Leaves pinnate, with oval leaflets and terminal, branched tendrils. Bracts toothed. Flowers solitary, almost stalkless in leaf axils. Corolla 1.5-2cm long pink to pinkish-violet. Calyx teeth about the same length as tube. Fruits to 7cm long, brown.
Flowering season: Jun-Sep
Habitat: Agricultural fields, footpaths
Distribution: Most of Europe; planted as fodder crop and widely distributed throughout the world.

3

Narrow-leaved Everlasting Pea*

(Pea Family) *Lathyrus sylvestris*

Hairless plant with many clambering winged stems, to 2m long. Leaves with winged stalks and 2 linear to lanceolate leaflets. Inflorescence long stemmed with 3-6 flowers. Calyx bell-shaped with 5 teeth of uneven length. Corolla 1.3-1.8cm long, pink to purple, often somewhat greenish. Pods 5-7cm long and 0.8-1.3cm wide. Seeds 4-5.5mm in diameter.
Flowering season: Jul-Aug
Habitat: Open woods, scrub
Distribution: Most of Europe, but absent from the far N of Europe, and most of Scotland and Ireland.

4

Spring Pea ✿ *Lathyrus vernus*

(Pea Family)

Mostly hairless plant growing to about 30cm tall. Stem erect, unbranched. Leaves pinnate, with 4-8 leaflets ending in a short point. Leaflets broad and lanceolate. Inflorescence long stalked. Flowers drooping. Corolla 1.5-2cm long, at first red, then blue and eventually turning greenish-blue. Calyx teeth of unequal length. Fruit to 6cm long, linear, hairless.
Flowering season: Apr-May
Habitat: Deciduous woodland; calcareous soils
Distribution: Most of Europe eastwards to Caucasus and Siberia. Absent from extreme N and W of Europe, including British Isles, but often grown as an early-flowering garden plant.

1
2|3
4

1

Bloody Crane's-bill* ❀ *Geranium sanguineum*

(Crane's-bill Family)

Upright hairy plant to 60cm tall. Stem spreading and much-branched. Leaves opposite and deeply pinnate with up to 7 lobes. Bracts small. Flowers often solitary, long-stemmed. Flower stalks and sepals with glandular hairs. Sepals 8-12mm long and pointed. Petals rather irregular and rounded. Fruit 3-4cm long.
Flowering season: May-Sep
Habitat: Rocky outcrops, dry grassland, scrub, woodland margins and dunes
Distribution: most of Europe; Caucasus; Turkey. In Britain mainly in W and N.

2

Herb-Robert* *Geranium robertianum*

(Crane's-bill Family)

Rather a spreading plant to 50cm tall, with an unpleasant smell and hairy stems and leaves. Stalked leaves opposite with 3-5 lobes. Lobes deeply separated. Flowers mostly in pairs, short-stalked. Flower stalks and calyx with glandular and non glandular hairs. Sepals 6-8mm long, erect, pointed. Petals 9-12mm long, rounded. Anthers orange. Fruit 0.5-1.5cm long.
Flowering season: May-Dec
Habitat: Woods, scrub, clearings, walls
Distribution: Europe; most of Asia; N America; N Africa.

3

Dove's-foot Crane's-bill* *Geranium molle*

(Crane's-bill Family)

Annual to about 40cm tall, with shallowly cut leaves, more or less round in outline. Flowers pink, 10-12mm across, with deeply notched petals.
Flowering season: Jun-Jul
Habitat: Hedges, banks, waste ground
Distribution: W and C Europe; common in Britain and Ireland.
Similar species: Small-flowered Crane's-bill°, *G. pusillum*, has small (to about 8mm across) pale pink-purple flowers with whitish centre, and more deeply divided leaves.

4

Common Stork's-bill* *Erodium cicutarium*

(Crane's-bill Family)

Hairy plant to 40cm tall. Leaves pinnate with deeply separated lobes. Inflorescence long-stalked, with a whitish stipule at base. Sepals 4-7mm long, with short point. Petals 5-9mm long, the two uppermost petals with a dark spot at the base. Fruit 3-4cm long.
Flowering season: May-Oct
Habitat: Cultivated fields, footpaths, waste ground, dry grassland, dunes
Distribution: Worldwide. In British Isles mainly on sandy soils.

1
2|3
4

1

Sticky Flax ⚘ ☒ *Linum viscosum*

(Flax Family)

Hairy plant with leafy stem, to 60cm tall. Leaves lanceolate, 3-5 veined, with glandular hairs at the margins. Sepals 6-9mm long, lanceolate, with glandular marginal hairs. Petals to 25mm long, pink, streaked blue. Fruit rounded, 3.5-4.5mm long

Flowering season: May-Jul

Habitat: Dry grassland, open pinewoods, woodland margins

Distribution: much of Europe, but absent from British Isles.

2

Burning Bush* ⚘ ☒ *Dictamnus albus*

(Rue Family)

Tall plant to 1.2m, smelling of cinnamon. Covered with black glands, especially towards the top of the plant. Leaves stalked, pinnate, with 7-11 finely-toothed leaflets. Flowers clustered in a terminal spike, weakly zygomorphic, to 5cm broad, 5-partite. Sepals 6-28mm long. Petals 2-3cm long, pink with dark veins. 4 petals grow upwards, the lower petals curved downwards. Fruit 1cm long, 5-partite.

Flowering season: May-Jun

Habitat: Dry slopes, open woodland, scrub

Distribution: C and S Europe; Asia. A garden plant only in the British Isles.

Note: Like all members of the Rutaceae (such as *Citrus* fruits) this species contains many essential oils, which are given off in such quantities on hot days that they fill the air surrounding the plants. These oils protect the plants from desiccation.

3

Common Mallow* *Malva sylvestris*

(Mallow Family)

Plant to 1.2m tall. Stem trailing or erect. Leaves stalked, with 3-7 ovate, toothed lobes. Flowers in groups in the leaf axils. Epicalyx with 2-3 lobes. Petals 2-3cm long, with dark veins. Fruits about 1cm broad. The individual nutlets have irregular wrinkles along the back, and indistinct radial stripes at the side.

Flowering season: May-Sep

Habitat: Footpaths, waste ground, roadsides, fields

Distribution: Virtually worldwide.

Similar species: Large-flowered Mallow ⚘, *M. alcea,* has stem leaves split almost to the base, and smooth nutlets with longitudinal ribs along the back. Musk Mallow°, *M. moschata,* has stem leaves divided almost to base. Nutlets thickly hairy along the back, smooth-sided.

NUTLET
Large-flowered Mallow

NUTLET
Musk Mallow

NUTLET
Common Mallow

1|2

3

1

Garland Flower ☠ ❀ ☒ *Daphne cneorum*

(Daphne Family)

Branched, somewhat hairy dwarf shrub growing to about 30cm tall. Leaves narrow and wedge-shaped or spoon-shaped, leathery, and remaining on the plant for several years. Dark green on both sides and evenly distributed around stem. Flowers in groups at the ends of the stems. Petals absent (their place being taken by pinkish red tube-shaped calyx with 4 spreading calyx lobes). Calyx tube thickly hairy on the outside. Fruit hairy.

Flowering season: May-Aug

Habitat: Dry slopes, heathy meadows, open pinewoods; mainly on calcareous soils

Distribution: C and S Europe. Not in British Isles.

Similar species: Other *Daphne* species occur in Europe, of which the most widespread is Mezereon° ❀ ☒, *D. mezereum*, with pink flowers on leafless twigs in January to March. Rare as a native in Britain, but commonly cultivated.

2

Purple-loosestrife* ❀ *Lythrum salicaria*

(Loosestrife Family)

Hairy plant to about 2m tall. Stem erect, angled, with many leaves. Leaves to 10cm long, lanceolate, stalkless, rounded towards the base. Lower leaves opposite or in whorls of 3. Middle leaves alternate or opposite. Upper leaves alternate. Inflorescence usually more than 10cm long. Flowers short-stalked, in clusters, in the axils of bracts. Calyx 5-7mm long, with 12 ribs. Epicalyx present with 6 teeth. 6 petals 8-12mm long, purplish red, violet, sometimes pink or rarely white. 12 stamens.

Flowering season: Jun-Sep

Habitat: Fens, ditches, river banks, pond margins

Distribution: Most of Europe; east to Japan; N Africa.

1
2

1

Rose-bay Willowherb* *Epilobium angustifolium*

(Willowherb Family)

Upright plant to 1.8m tall with leafy stems. Leaves alternate, lanceolate, with several veins, to 15cm long, up to 2cm broad, margins curving downwards. Upper side of leaf dark green, underside bluish green. Flowers 4-partite, to 3cm wide, weakly zygomorphic, clustered in a terminal raceme. Sepals narrow, almost as long as petals, pinkish. Petals of uneven size, rounded, spreading. Capsule to 5cm long, hairy and often suffused with red.

Flowering season: Jun-Sep

Habitat: Clearings, footpaths, tall-herb communities, river and lake banks, waste ground, scrub

Distribution: Most of Europe; Asia; N America.

Note: this species is characterised by its somewhat zygomorphic flowers and is thus easily identified. For this and other reasons it is placed in its own sub-genus *Chamaenerion*. There are only two other species in Europe belonging to this group. These are almost exclusively confined to the Alps and are low-growing species of river gravel.

2

Great Willowherb* *Epilobium hirsutum*

(Willowherb Family)

Hairy plant to 1.5m tall with rounded, leafy stems. Leaves lanceolate to elliptical and toothed. In the lower part of the stem opposite and often encircling the stem, higher up alternate. Flowers solitary, in the axils of the upper stem leaves. 4 sepals 8-10mm long, pointed. 4 petals, 12-18mm long. Stamens and style erect. Stigma star-shaped. Fruit to 5cm long.

Flowering season: Jun-Sep

Habitat: River and stream banks, ditches, tall-herb communities

Distribution: Most of Europe; large parts of Asia; N Africa.

Similar species: Hoary Willowherb°, *E. parviflorum*. Corolla 6-9mm long, pale pink, leaves not encircling stem. Similar habitats.

3

Broad-leaved Willowherb* *Epilobium montanum*

(Willowherb Family)

Plant to 1 metre. Stem branched in upper part and covered there with glandular hairs. Leaves lanceolate to elliptical, toothed; in the lower half of the stem these are opposite and almost stalkless. Flowers solitary in the axils of upper stem leaves. Sepals pointed. Petals 8-12mm long. Fruit with curved appressed hairs and upright glandular hairs.

Flowering Season: Jul-Sep

Habitat: Woods, hedges, gardens

Distribution: Most of Europe; eastwards to Siberia.

Similar species: Spear-leaved Willowherb°, *E. lanceolatum,* has obvious leaf-stalks, 4-10mm long, and alternate upper leaves. W and C Europe, north to S England and S Wales.

Note: All willow-herbs are characterised by 4-partite flowers and long inferior ovaries developing into capsules splitting into 4 valves and releasing abundant seeds with a plume of long hairs for wind dispersal.

1
2|3

1

Bell Heather* ❀ *Erica cinerea*

(Heather Family)

Low growing shrub to 50cm. Similar to Cross-leaved Heath, but hairless and with purplish flowers. Leaves in 3s, hairless and dark green. Flowers pink-purple, in small groups, not terminal clusters.
Flowering season: Jun-Sep
Habitat: Mainly on drier acid soils of heaths and moors
Distribution: Throughout, but not in far N. In British Isles throughout, but local in C England and C Ireland.

2

Cross-leaved Heath* ❀ *Erica tetralix*

(Heather Family)

Dwarf shrub to 70cm tall with densely hairy twigs. Leaves 3-5mm long, needlelike, evergreen, 3 or 4 to a whorl, edged with red topped glandular hairs. Flowers clustered in heads. Corolla 6-8mm long narrowly oval. Sepals green about a third as long as the corolla. Stamens hidden inside the corolla.
Flowering season: Jun-Sep
Habitat: Bogs and wet, acid, sandy soils
Distribution: N and W Europe; common in British Isles.

3

Cranberry* *Vaccinium oxycoccos*

(Heather Family)

Dwarf shrub with creeping, rather threadlike stems up to 1m long. Leaves opposite, evergreen, oval to lanceolate up to 1cm long and rolled downwards at margins. Flowers solitary on long slender stems. Corolla split almost to the base, the 4 corolla lobes bent backwards, 5-7mm long. 4 semicircular sepals. Stamens forming a tube. Fruit a round, red berry up to 1cm across.
Flowering season: Jun-Aug
Habitat: Raised bogs
Distribution: N and C Europe; Asia; N America. In British Isles commonest in N England and S and C Scotland.

4

Heather* ❀ *Calluna vulgaris*

(Heather Family)

Shrub up to 1m tall. Leaves evergreen, arranged in fours and overlapping each other rather like roof tiles. Flowers clustered along one side of stem. 4-lobed green epicalyx. Sepals pink, 4mm long. Petals 2mm long and fused for two thirds of their length.
Flowering season: Aug-Oct
Habitat: Heaths, mires, pinewoods
Distribution: Europe. The most widespread "heath" in Europe.

1

2|3

4

1

Bird's-eye Primrose* ✿ ☒ *Primula farinosa*

(Primrose Family)

Plant to 30cm with basal leaves. Leaves somewhat rolled when young, spoon-shaped and weakly wrinkled and green on the upper side, on the underside greyish-white and mealy. Leaf margins usually weakly serrated. Flowers 10-15mm long, flowerstalk also mealy. Corollas 5-lobed, 8-15mm across, pink with a yellow throat. Sepals 4-6mm long, about as long as the corolla tube.

Flowering season: May-Jul

Habitat: Fens, grassland, wet screes; always on calcareous soils

Distribution: Alps and Alpine foothills, Arctic and other European mountains; Asia; N America. Also grows in Northern England and Scotland.

2

Cyclamen ✿ ☒ *Cyclamen purpurascens*

(Primrose Family)

Plant to 20cm tall with broad oval or kidney-shaped leaves lasting for several seasons. Leaves somewhat fleshy and shiny above with paler markings and weakly serrated edge; undersides purple. Flowers solitary, drooping, scented, with dark central markings. Corolla lobes to 20mm long, angled sharply backwards. Flower stalks long, rolling up from the tip in fruit.

Flowering season: Jun-Sep

Habitat: Woods, scrub, open grassland; always on calcareous soils

Distribution: Hills and mountains of C and S Europe.

Similar species: The widespread Sowbread°, *C. hederifolium,* with pale pink or white flowers, is possibly native in woods in SE England. Other species are commonly cultivated.

3

Scarlet Pimpernel* ☠ *Anagallis arvensis*

(Primrose Family)

Hairless annual plant to 10cm with straggling rectangular stems. Leaves opposite, to 2cm long, oval to lanceolate, pointed and stalkless. Flowers in the leaf axils, solitary, long-stalked and 5-partite. Sepals 4-5mm long, joined together at the base. Corolla 5-7mm long, divided almost to the base, usually red, sometimes blue and rarely pink. Corolla lobes widely spread, entire, with glandular hairs at the edges. Fruit a 4-5mm long capsule, opening around the middle.

Flowering season: Jun-Oct

Habitat: Cultivated land, waste ground

Distribution: Almost worldwide.

Similar species: Blue Pimpernel°, *A. foemina*. Corolla always blue, corolla lobes finely toothed.

1
2
3

1 Chiltern Gentian* ☒ *Gentianella germanica*

(Gentian Family)

Much-branched plant to about 50cm tall. Leaves oval and pointed. Flowers violet, mostly 5-partite, hairy in the throat and. Calyx tube-shaped with lanceolate, smooth tips.

Flowering season: May-Oct. *Habitat:* poor grassland, pastures, fens
Distribution: W and C Europe. Local on chalk in S England.
Similar species: Field Gentian°, *G. campestris*, with 4-partite flowers is found in similar habitats from N Europe to the Pyrenees and Alps. In British Isles commonest in N and W. The commonest member of this genus in the British Isles is Felwort°, *G. amarella* (see p 16).

2 Thrift* ✿ *Armeria maritima*

(Sea-lavender Family)

Plant to 40cm tall. Leaves in basal rosette, narrowly linear and fringed with hairs. Inflorescence a terminal, dense cluster on leafless stem. Bracts joined together to form a tube below inflorescence.

Flowering season: Jun-Aug
Habitat: Coasts, salt marshes, sand; also on heavy metal soils
Distribution: Throughout Europe, mainly coastal in Scandinavia and British Isles.

3 Common Sea-lavender* *Limonium vulgare*

(Sea-lavender Family)

Hairless plant to 50cm tall. Leaves basal, stalked, obovate, with rather stiff margins. Stem branched with dense clusters of flowers. Flowers small, pinkish violet.

Flowering season: Aug-Sep. *Habitat:* Sea coasts, salt marshes.
Distribution: Coasts of Europe and N Africa.

4 Common Centaury* ☒ *Centaurium erythraea*

(Gentian Family)

Biennial, hairless plant to 30cm. Lower leaves arranged in a rosette and narrowly oval. Stem leaves opposite and oval. Flowers pink, in a loose branched inflorescence. Corolla lobes oval and opening out into a starshaped flower.

Flowering season: Jul-Sep. *Habitat:* Meadows, clearings, dry slopes
Distribution: Europe; Asia; N Africa. Common throughout British Isles, except Scotland, where less common.
Similar species: Lesser Centaury°, *C. pulchellum*, a slenderer plant, is annual. It lacks a basal rosette and has a muchbranched stem and pointed corolla lobes. Damp meadows and fields.

5 Sea Bindweed* ☒ *Calystegia soldanella*

(Bindweed Family)

Hairless plant to 15cm tall with creeping stems. Leaves alternate, kidney-shaped and somewhat fleshy. Flowers stalked, with 2 oval bracts at base. Corolla to 5cm across, funnel-shaped, pink, with 5 white stripes.

Flowering season: May-Aug *Habitat:* Coastal sand and dunes
Distribution: Coasts of most of Europe, including British Isles, except N Scotland; N to Denmark.

1|2
3
4|5

1

Wall Germander* ❀ *Teucrium chamaedrys*

(Mint Family)

Plant to 30cm tall, with a woody base to the stem. Stem hairy. Leaves oval, toothed, with musty smell when crushed, about as long as flowers. Inflorescence nodding to one side. Flowers mostly clustered in the axils of the upper leaves and with short stalks. Calyx 6-8mm long, more or less regularly 5-lobed, weakly 2-lipped and hairy. Corolla 1-1.5cm long with only the lower lip obvious (upper lip divided into 2 and the lobes deflected to the sides).

Flowering season: Jul-Aug

Habitat: Rocky outcrops, dry grassland, open woodland

Distribution: Much of Europe; Turkey; N Africa. Doubtfully native in Britain, naturalized from gardens.

2

Vervain* ☒ *Verbena officinalis*

(Vervain Family)

Plant to 80cm tall. Stem rectangular, branched above and roughly hairy along the ridges, otherwise hairless. Leaves opposite, lower leaves scarcely divided and only roughly toothed, middle leaves 3 or more times divided, upper leaves again only toothed. Inflorescence a thin, loose spike with glandular hairs in the axils and on calyx. Corolla 3-5mm long, tube-like lower down, with a 5-lobed, 2-lipped opening. Calyx tube-shaped with 4 to 5 lobes and 2mm long.

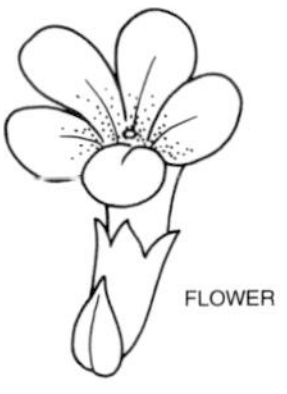

Flowering season: Jul-Sep

Habitat: Footpath edges, wasteland, meadows

Distribution: Most of Europe, including Britain; much of Asia; N Africa.

3

Red Hemp-nettle* *Galeopsis angustifolia*

(Mint Family)

Annual plant to 30cm tall. Leaves narrow, lanceolate, entire or weakly toothed and covered in hairs. Flowers in whorled inflorescences in the axils of the upper leaves. Bracts bristly and pointed. Calyx narrowly bell-shaped, with 10 veins and 5 pointed teeth of equal length. Corolla tube 1-2cm long. Upper lip entire, hood-shaped. Lower lip 3-lobed; central part with 2 lobes, on each side toothed at the base.

Flowering season: Jun-Oct

Habitat: Waste ground, railway tracks, stony places, gravel

Distribution: Much of Europe, especially towards the S. In Britain mainly in SE England.

1

2|3

1

Spotted Dead-nettle* ✿ *Lamium maculatum*

(Mint Family)

Perennial plant, to 50cm tall with 4-angled stem. Leaves stalked, opposite, oval and toothed. Calyx narrowly bell-shaped, 5-veined. Corolla 2-3cm long, corolla tube opening upwards and curved. Lower lip 3-lobed, spotted. *Flowering season:* Apr-Oct. *Habitat:* Woods, scrub, footpaths, waste ground *Distribution:* Most of Europe, W Asia, Turkey.
Note: In Britain this species, which is commonly grown in gardens and often naturalized, usually has leaves with silver blotches.

2

Red Dead-nettle* *Lamium purpureum*

(Mint Family)

Annual plant, to 20cm tall with 4-angled stem. Leaves opposite, stalked, heartshaped and toothed. Calyx narrowly bell-shaped. Corolla 0.8-1.2cm long, with narrow straight tube. Lower lip 3-lobed, with threadlike teeth at the sides. Anthers violet, with white hairs.
Flowering season: Apr-Oct. *Habitat:* Agricultural fields, gardens, waste ground. *Distribution:* Europe; Asia.

3

Betony* *Stachys officinalis*

(Mint Family)

Perennial plant, to 70cm tall. Leaves stalked, narrowly oval, with heart shaped base, toothed. Calyx 5-7mm long, with 5 teeth, edged with bristles. Corolla 1-1.5cm long. Upper lip flat, almost straight when seen from the side. Anthers sticking straight out.
Flowering season: Jul-Sep. *Habitat:* dry grassland, meadows, open woods *Distribution:* most of Europe; W Asia; N Africa. Common in England and Wales; rarer in Ireland and N Scotland.

4

Marsh Woundwort* *Stachys palustris*

(Mint Family)

Perennial plant, to 1m tall with 4-angled, sparsely hairy stem. Leaves heartshaped at the base, stalkless or with very short stalks, and narrowly lanceolate. Calyx 7-10mm long, bell-shaped, with short hairs. Corolla 14-17mm long, with short hairs on the outside. Upper lip entire, curved into a hood shape. Lower lip 3-lobed with dark spots. Anthers bending outwards to the sides. *Flowering season:* Jun-Sep. *Habitat:* banks, wet meadows, ditches, wet fields *Distribution:* most of Europe; Asia; N America.

5

Hedge Woundwort* *Stachys sylvatica*

(Mint Family)

Perennial plant, to 1m tall with rectangular hairy stems. Foliage has characteristic unpleasant smell. Leaves stalked, oval, roughly toothed and pointed. Calyx 4-7mm long, covered in thick hairs. Corolla 1.2-1.5cm, reddish-brown, hairy on the outside. Lower lip 3-lobed, with dark spots. *Flowering season:* Jun-Sep. *Habitat:* woods, scrub, clearings *Distribution:* Most of Europe; much of Asia.

1|2

3

4|5

1 Black Horehound* *Ballota nigra*

(Mint Family)

Thickly hairy plant with unpleasant smell, growing to about 1m tall. Leaves opposite, stalked, oval and toothed. Calyx funnel-shaped, 10-veined. Calyx teeth long with bristly tips. Corolla 1-1.4cm. Long straight upper lip, with edges curved downwards. Lower lip 3-lobed and white spotted.

Flowering season: May-Oct

Habitat: Footpaths, waste places, hedges

Distribution: Most of Europe. Absent from extreme N and W of Europe, but common in England and Wales.

2 Water Mint* *Mentha aquatica*

(Mint Family)

Aromatic plant to 80cm tall with characteristic minty smell. Stem almost hairless or weakly hairy. Leaves short-stalked, oval, toothed. Flowers stalked, at the end of stem or in the axils of the uppermost leaves, in fairly dense clusters. Calyx tube-shaped and 5-lobed. Corolla 5-7mm long with a ring of hairs in the tube and 4 even corolla lobes. 4 stamens extending outside corolla.

Flowering season: Jul-Oct

Habitat: Banks, wet meadows, wet woodland, marshes

Distribution: Most of Europe; most of Asia; N and S Africa. Usually on calcareous soils in British Isles.

3 Marjoram* *Origanum vulgare*

(Mint Family)

Hairy, aromatic plant to 50cm tall. Leaves opposite, oval, lower leaves stalked. Flowers clustered into heads at the ends of stems and also in whorls lower down. Bracts 3-6mm long, purple. Calyx bell-shaped, with 13 veins, 2.5-3.5mm long, with 5 triangular even teeth. Corolla pink, weakly 2-lipped, 4-7mm long.

Flowering season: Jul-Oct

Habitat: Dry grassland, dry open oak and pine woods, sunny woodland margins and hedges

Distribution: Most of Europe, Asia.

4 Wild Basil* *Clinopodium vulgare*

(Mint Family)

Spright, hairy, almost unscented plant, growing to 60cm tall. Leaves opposite, oval, short stalked. Flowers short stalked, in dense heads in the axils of the upper leaves. Calyx tube-like, 13-veined, 2-lipped, 8-10mm long. Corolla 10-14mm long, pale purple, 2-lipped with short flat upper lip and longer 3-lobed lower lip.

Flowering season: Jul-Oct

Habitat: Open woods, woodland margins, shaded meadows, scrub

Distribution: Europe; N Asia; N America.

1|2
3
4

1

Corn Mint* *Mentha arvensis*

(Mint Family)

To about 60cm tall, with only slight minty smell. The flowers are in clusters lower down the stem, not at the top. Flowers lilac, corolla hairy, stamens protruding. Calyx hairy, with short teeth.

Flowering season: May-Oct

Habitat: Arable fields, woodland clearings, waste ground. Prefers rather drier places than most mints

Distribution: Throughout Europe, in Britain mainly in lowlands.

2

Round-leaved Mint* *Mentha sauveolens*

(Mint Family)

Hairy unstalked rounded leaves, felty beneath. Flowers in spikes up to 5cm long.

Flowering season: Aug-Sep

Habitat: Ditches and streams

Distribution: Europe N to Holland as a native, widely naturalized. In Britain, mainly S W England and Wales.

Note: Other garden mints, often hybrid in origin, are widely grown and naturalized. One of the commonest in Britain is Spearmint*❀, *M. spicata.*

3

Large Thyme* *Thymus pulegioides*

(Mint Family)

Aromatic, creeping plant with stems up to 40cm long, either growing along the ground or arched upwards. Flowering stems noticeably 4-angled, mostly hairy only on the ridges. Leaves opposite, oval to spoon-shaped, narrowing towards stalk and with long bristles at base. Flowers in groups in the axils of the upper leaves, either in whorls or in denser heads. Calyx noticeably 2-lipped. Corolla small, 2-lipped, 3-6mm long.

Flowering season: Jun-Oct

Habitat: Dry grassland, footpaths, scrub, walls

Distribution: C and N Europe (except far N & NW). In Britain common only in the S.

Similar species: Breckland Thyme°, *T. serpyllum,* has long, creeping rounded stems, hairy on all sides and narrowly lanceolate leaves. Only in sandy parts of C Europe. Also a rare British species, found in the East Anglian Breckland. Wild Thyme°, *T. praecox,* has long, creeping stems, rounded flowering stems and an even distribution of hairs. Leaves rounded to oval. Common in Britain. In C Europe mainly in the mountains.

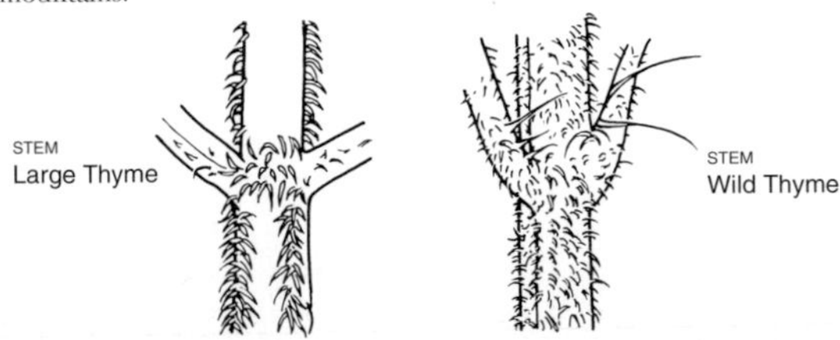

1|2

3

1

Foxglove* ☠ ❀

Digitalis purpurea

(Figwort Family)

Plant to 1.5 m tall. Stem unbranched, upright, covered with grey felty hairs. Leaves oval to lanceolate, toothed, lower leaves stalked, forming a rosette which often dies off by flowering time. Upper leaves stalkless. Inflorescence a raceme, flowers nodding to one side. Calyx 5-lobed. Sepals oval, with glandular hairs which are also present on the flower stalks and the upper part of the stem. Corolla drooping downwards, with an inflated tube and short, 2-lobed margin. Lower lip 3-lobed, longer than upper lip (to 5cm), dark red inside with paler specks.

Flowering season: Jun-Aug

Habitat: Open woods, clearings, footpaths; on acid soils

Distribution: Much of Europe; often cultivated and naturalized.

Note: This species is a typical biennial. After germination a basal rosette develops in the first year and the flowering stem grows up from this in the second year. The plant normally then dies after the seeds have been dispersed.

2

Bittersweet, Woody Nightshade* ☠

(Nightshade Family)

Solanum dulcamara

Plant to 2m tall. Stem woody towards base. Leaves oval to lanceolate, often heartshaped at the base or with 1 or 2 lobes, otherwise entire. Calyx 5-toothed; teeth roundly ovate. Corolla 0.8-1.2cm across, fused at the base and opening into 5 lobes. Stamens short, anthers joined together into a tube from which the style projects. Ovary superior. Fruit a bright red berry.

Flowering season: Jun-Sep

Habitat: Hedges, wet woodland, banks, clearings

Distribution: Europe; much of Asia.

3

Small Toadflax*

Chaenorhinum minus

(Figwort Family)

Annual plant to 30cm tall, covered with glandular hairs. Leaves narrowly lanceolate to linear, lower ones somewhat broader and opposite, the upper ones alternate. Flowers long-stalked, solitary, in the leaf axils. Corolla 0.3-0.6cm long, pale violet to grey violet, with yellow spot on palate. In the form of a short 2-lipped tube widening towards the front with a spur at the back. Upper lip flat, lower lip 3-lobed. Spur half as long as the rest of the corolla, and straight.

Flowering season: May-Oct

Habitat: Gardens, fields, footpaths, waste ground

Distribution: Europe; Turkey; N Africa.

1

2|3

1

Ivy-leaved Toadflax* ✿ *Cymbalaria muralis*

(Figwort Family)

Creeping, hairless plant with threadlike rooting stems. Leaves long-stalked, 5-7 lobed. Flowers long-stalked, solitary in the leaf axils. Corolla 0.6-0.8cm long, pale violet with yellow spot on palate, 2-lipped and spurred at base. Upper lip flat. Lower lip 3-lobed, with a projection closing the flower.
Flowering season: Jun-Sep
Habitat: Rocks, walls, scree, river gravel; calcareous soils
Distribution: Most of Europe; N Africa; W Asia; N America. Introduced and widespread in British Isles.
Note: After flowering, the flower stalks grow downwards into the surrounding soil, thus increasing the likelihood of germination.

2

Marsh Lousewort* ☒ *Pedicularis palustris*

(Figwort Family)

Plant to 70cm tall, with a single erect, branched stem. Leaves deeply pinnate, with toothed lobes. Flowers solitary in the upper leaf axils. Calyx tube-shaped, 2-lobed. Corolla 1.5-2cm long. Upper lip hood-shaped; lower lip flat and hairy.
Flowering season: May-Aug
Habitat: wet meadows, fens
Distribution: Europe, except Mediterranean region; Asia; N America.
Similar species: Lousewort*, ☒. *P. sylvatica,* has many stems with flowers all the way down the main stem, and a hairless lower lip, shorter than the upper lip. Woodland clearings and wet heath.

3

Red Bartsia* *Odontites verna*

(Figwort Family)

Plant to 50cm tall with lanceolate toothed leaves. Flowers solitary, in upper leaf axils. Calyx 4-8mm long, hairy. Corolla 8-12mm long, thickly hairy. Upper lip longer than lower lip. Stamens protruding beyond upper lip.
Flowering season: May-Sep
Habitat: Fields, footpath edges, pasture, grassland
Distribution: Most of Europe; much of Asia.

4

Common Valerian* *Valeriana officinalis*

(Valerian Family)

Erect plant growing to 1.8m tall. Leaves opposite. Basal leaves large and pinnate; stem leaves somewhat smaller. Flowers in terminal cluster. Corolla 3-6mm long, pink to whitish, tube-shaped at the base, becoming funnel-shaped and 3-4 lobed. Calyx with thickened margin. Ovary inferior.
Flowering season: May-Sep
Habitat: Open woods, tall herb communities, wet meadows, ditches, river banks
Distribution: Most of Europe.

BASAL LEAF
Common Valerian

1

2

3|4

1

Teasel* ❀ *Dipsacus fullonum*

(Teasel Family)

To 2m tall. Stem, and also sometimes lower midrib of leaf, spiny. Basal leaves to 40cm long, short-stalked, oval and toothed. Stem leaves opposite, sometimes joined together at the base, lanceolate, toothed or entire. Flower head long, oval or cylindrical. Bracts in 2 rows, spiny. Flowers in the axils of the bracts, which extend beyond the flowers. Corolla 4-lobed. Corolla tube about 1cm long. Calyx 4-lobed.

Flowering season: Jul-Aug

Habitat: Footpath edges, wasteground, river banks

Distribution: Most of Europe; S W Asia; N Africa; Canary Islands.

2

Field Scabious* *Knautia arvensis*

(Teasel Family)

Plant to 1m tall, with stiffly hairy stem. Lower leaves lanceolate, entire or toothed, sometimes pinnate. Middle and upper leaves mostly pinnate. Flower heads flat, with large ray florets. Bracts in several rows. Corolla tube-shaped at the base, 4-lobed above. Calyx with 8-10 hairs, each 2-3mm long. Fruit 5-6mm, densely hairy.

Flowering season: Jul-Sep

Habitat: Meadows, dry slopes, footpath edges, fields

Distribution: Most of Europe; W Asia.

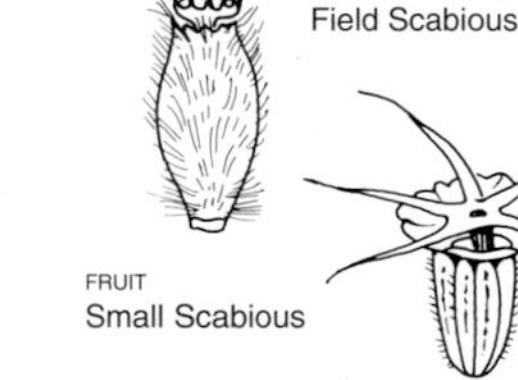

3

Small Scabious* *Scabiosa columbaria*

(Teasel Family)

Like a smaller version of Field Scabious, to about 70cm tall, with flower heads about 1.5-3cm across. When fruiting, the honeycomb texture of the heads is distinctive. Fruit 3mm, crowned by persistent calyx with 5 blackish narrow teeth.

Flowering season: Jul-Aug

Habitat: Dry chalk grassland, banks

Distribution: C and W Europe, N to Britain and S Sweden. In Britain throughout England and Wales, but not in most of Scotland. Absent from Ireland.

1
2|3

1

Hemp-agrimony* *Eupatorium cannabinum*

(Daisy Family)

To 1.5m tall. Leaves opposite, with 3-5 lanceolate, toothed segments. Flower heads each with 4-6 florets, arranged in a branched terminal inflorescence. Bracts 4.5-6mm long, cylindrical. All florets tubular.

Flowering season: Jul-Sep

Habitat: Wet woodland, riverbanks, pond margins, tall herb communities

Distribution: Most of Europe; W Asia; N Africa.

2

Sea Aster* *Aster tripolium*

(Daisy Family)

Virtually hairless plant to 1m tall. Leaves linear-lanceolate, often fleshy. Flowering heads 2-2.5cm across. Involucre 6-8mm tall. Bracts in 2-3 rows. Ray florets 2.5mm across, 10mm long, pinkish-violet to light blue, sometimes absent. Tube florets yellow.

Flowering season: Jun-Sep

Habitat: Wet saltmarsh, salty meadows, ditches

Distribution: Coasts of Europe, occasionally inland; Asia. Common around Britain.

3

Welted Thistle* *Carduus acanthoides*

(Daisy Family)

Plant to 1.5m tall. Upper stem with white felty hairs. Leaves deeply pinnate and spiny. Leaf bases extended down stem. Flower heads 1.5-2.5cm across. Corollas tube-shaped, 5-lobed. Pappus hairs rough, not feathery.

Flowering season: Jun-Oct

Habitat: Footpath margins, grassland, wasteground

Distribution: Much of Europe, N to Sweden and Britain.

4

Slender Thistle* *Carduus tenuiflorus*

(Daisy Family)

Erect plant to 1m tall, with narrow branches. Stems with broad wings. Flower heads cylindrical, to about 20mm long and about 5-10mm wide, in dense, terminal clusters. Florets pale pink or pale purple.

Flowering season: May-Aug

Habitat: Waste ground, dry grassland, often near the sea

Distribution: W Europe, N to British Isles and Holland.

5

Musk Thistle* *Carduus nutans*

(Daisy Family)

Plant to 1.2m tall. Stem with white felty hairs, especially at the top. Leaves ascending almost to flower heads, deeply pinnate and spiny. Leaf margins extended as wings down stem. Flower heads 3-8cm broad and high, nodding to one side, sweet scented. Outer bracts spiny and broad at base. Corollas tube-shaped at the base, funnel-shaped above, 5-lobed. Pappus hairs rough, not feathery.

Flowering season: Jul-Sep

Habitat: Footpath margins, waste ground, pasture

Distribution: Much of Europe; Turkey; Caucasus; N Africa; W Asia. Rare in Ireland; common in England and Wales; less common in Scotland.

1|2
3
4|5

1

Marsh Thistle*

Cirsium palustre

(Daisy Family)

Hairy plant to 1.5m tall. Stem branched only towards the top and winged over its entire length by the spiny leaf margins. Leaves longish, pinnately divided, with triangular spiny lobes and spiny toothed margins. Leaves green above, hairy below, young leaves in particular with white felty hairs. Inflorescences clustered. Involucre 1-1.5cm long, purple, covered with felty hairs. Bracts with weakly spiny points. Fruit pappus feathery.

Flowering season: Jul-Sep

Habitat: Damp meadows, marshes, fens

Distribution: Europe; N Asia; N Africa.

Similar species: Dwarf Thistle*, *C. acaule,* is a stemless thistle with a rosette of basal leaves. Inflorescence solitary in the centre of the rosette. Involucre 2-3cm long, reddish brown. Bracts with weak spines. Dry to damp meadows and heaths. C and S Europe N to S Scandinavia and N England. Usually on chalk or limestone in England.

WHOLE PLANT
Dwarf Thistle

2

Spear Thistle*

Cirsium vulgare

(Daisy Family)

Robust, spiny plant growing to 1.5m tall. Stem somewhat branched and with rather interrupted spiny wings. Leaves stiff, pinnate, with lanceolate lobes ending in a sharp yellowish spine; green above and prickly below, covered with thick white felty hairs. Inflorescences solitary at the ends of stems, large. Involucre 3-5cm long, rounded. Bracts numerous, prickly and outwardly directed. Pappus feathery.

Flowering season: Aug-Oct

Habitat: Waste ground, footpaths, clearings

Distribution: Europe; W Asia.

Note: The Spear Thistle is one of the most stately of our native *Cirsium* species. The Woolly Thistle*, *C. eriophorum,* is still more impressive. It has flower heads to 7cm across and a white woolly involucre. All species of *Cirsium* can be distinguished from the genus *Carduus* by their feathery pappus hairs.

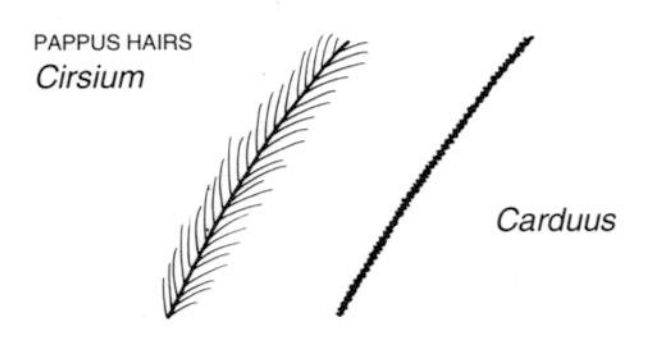

1
2

1 Creeping Thistle* *Cirsium arvense*

(Daisy Family)

Plant to 1.5m tall, with unwinged stem. Leaves hairless above, either hairless or covered in thick white felty hairs beneath. Leaves entire or divided to just over the midpoint, with spiny lobes. Involucre 1-2cm long and covered with weblike hairs, reddish violet in colour. Bracts with linear glands, outer ones with short, somewhat blunt thorns. Corolla 12-18cm long, pale violet, the upper part divided almost to the base. Fruits about 3mm long, brown, without spots. Pappus 2-3cm long with feathery hairs.

Flowering season: Jul-Oct

Habitat: Fields, waste ground, footpaths, clearings

Distribution: Europe; Asia; N Africa.

2 Brook Thistle *Cirsium rivulare*

(Daisy Family)

Thornless plant to 1m tall, with upright, unbranched stem covered in thick felty hairs towards top. Stem lacking wings. Upper stem leaves small and rather few. Lower leaves large and lanceolate with winged stalks, almost entire or deeply divided; green beneath. Inflorescences in groups of 2 to 4 or solitary. Involucre 1.5-2.5cm long, suffused with red and covered in felty hairs. Bracts with narrowly oval glands, the outer ones with short, blunt thorns. Corollas 1.5-2cm long, red. Fruits 4-5mm long, brownish. Pappus 1-1.5cm long, white and feathery.

Flowering season: May-Jun

Habitat: Marshy meadows, fens, river banks

Distribution: C Europe, particularly in the mountains.

Similar species: Meadow Thistle°☒, *C. dissectum,* is locally common in fens in S Britain and Ireland. It has similar flower heads, though mostly solitary, and grows in damp peaty soils. Tuberous Thistle°, *C. tuberosum,* is also similar but the leaves are much more divided. A rare and declining species in S Britain.

3 Greater Burdock * *Arctium lappa* agg.

(Daisy Family)

Plant to 1.5m tall. Leaves broad and oval, to 50cm long, green above, with felty hairs beneath. Flower heads 1.5-3cm across. Outer bracts of involucre with hooked spines, inner ones with straight spines. Florets all tubular. Outer corollas purple. Achenes 5-5.5mm long. Pappus 1-3mm long. The fruiting heads with their hooked bracts (burrs) are dispersed by animals.

Flowering season: Jul-Sep

Habitat: Footpaths, waste ground, river banks, scrub

Distribution: Most of Europe except far N, E to the Altai mountains. Common in British Isles.

Note: The species of burdock are difficult to distinguish from each other, though the genus is unmistakable.

1|2
3

1 Greater Knapweed* *Centaurea scabiosa*

(Daisy Family)

Plant to 1m tall with stalked, toothed basal leaves and unstalked upper stem leaves. Involucre 2-2.5cm across. Bracts with triangular blackish-brown appendages. Florets asymmetrical and tubular, larger towards the outside of the head.

Flowering season: Jun-Sep

Habitat: Meadows, footpaths, open woods

Distribution: Most of Europe; Asia.

2 Common Knapweed* *Centaurea nigra*

(Daisy Family)

A hairy plant to about 65cm tall, with tough, grooved stems and mostly undivided leaves. The flower heads are relatively small, tightly-packed, red-purple, opening from rather hard buds, with no larger florets towards the outside and surrounded by dark brown bracts.

Flowering season: Jun-Sep

Habitat: Grassland, roadsides, hedges, cliffs

Distribution: Mainly W Europe, N to C Scandinavia. Common throughout the British Isles.

3 Brown Knapweed* *Centaurea jacea*

(Daisy Family)

Differs from Common Knapweed most obviously in its larger heads with spreading, asymmetrical florets, and pale brown involucral bracts.

Flowering season: Jun-Oct

Habitat: Meadows, open woods

Distribution: Europe; Asia; N Africa. Very rare and only introduced in British Isles.

4 Saw-wort* *Serrulata tinctoria*

(Daisy Family)

Plant to 1m tall with undivided, elliptical, stalked basal leaves and pinnate, unstalked upper leaves. Involucre 1.5cm tall. Bracts lacking appendages and violet-red at the tip. Corolla tube-shaped and 5-lobed.

Flowering season: Jul-Aug

Habitat: Damp meadows, open woods

Distribution: most of Europe; Asia; N Africa.

5 Prenanthes *Prenanthes purpurea*

(Daisy Family)

Plant to 1.5m tall with milky juice. Leaves long, lower ones pinnate, with winged stalks. Upper leaves with heart-shaped base encircling stem. Flower heads 2-5 flowered, nodding. Involucre 1-1.5cm long; bracts in 2 rows.

Flowering season: Jul-Sep

Habitat: Woods, tall-herb communities, especially in the mountains

Distribution: Most of Europe, but absent from British Isles.

1|2
3
4|5

1 Arrowhead* ❀ *Sagittaria sagittifolia*

(Water-plantain Family)

Hairless water plant to 1m tall. First leaves to appear are grass-like and up to 1m long, floating in the water. These are followed by characteristically arrow-shaped leaves which grow out above the water surface in the flowering season. Flowers 1.5-2cm across, single sexed, in whorls, the lower whorls containing male and female flowers, the upper ones only male flowers. Outer perianth segments green and sepal-like, inner ones twice as large, and white with a red base.

Flowering season: Jun-Aug

Habitat: Still or slow flowing water to 50cm deep, river banks

Distribution: most of Europe; W Asia.

2 Water-plantain* ❀ *Alisma plantago-aquatica*

(Water-plantain Family)

Hairless plant to 1m tall. Leaves stalked, oval to lanceolate, rounded or heart-shaped at the base and growing up out of the water. The flowers, which open in the afternoon, have 3 green outer perianth segments, and 3 white inner perianth segments. The latter are 4-6mm long and rounded. Style almost straight, arising from below the middle of each carpel.

Flowering season: Jun-Aug

Habitat: Standing or slow flowing water to 15cm deep

Distribution: Worldwide.

Similar species: Narrow-leaved Water-plantain*, *A. lanceolatum,* has flowers which open in the morning and leaves narrowing towards the base. Style arising from above middle of carpels.

3 Water-soldier* ☒ *Stratiotes aloides*

(Frogbit Family)

Half submerged, mostly free-floating plant. Leaves sword-shaped, triangular, stiff, with sharp saw-like margins and up to 40cm long. Male and female flowers on separate plants and surrounded by a spathe. 3 outer perianth segments green, calyx-like; 3 inner segments white and about 2cm long.

Flowering season: May-Aug

Habitat: Warm, sheltered standing water

Distribution: Much of Europe; W Asia. Local in Britain, where only female plants occur.

4 Frogbit* ☒ *Hydrocharis morsus-ranae*

(Frogbit Family)

Plant with floating leaves (like those of a small water-lily), rooting in the mud. Sends out runners from which new rosettes develop. Leaves to 6cm across. Male and female flowers on separate plants and protected by spathe. 3 outer perianth segments calyxlike, green or pink. 3 inner perianth segments white with yellow at base and about 1.5cm long.

Flowering season: Jun-Aug

Habitat: Still, sheltered waters

Distribution: Most of Europe; Asia.

1|2
3
4

1 St Bernard's Lily ❀ ☒ *Anthericum liliago*

(Lily Family)

Hairless plant to 80cm tall with grass-like leaves up to 25cm long. Inflorescence a raceme. Individual flowers arise from axils of small bracts. 6 perianth segments all alike, 1.5-3cm long, widest at the midpoint. 6 stamens. Ovary superior. Fruit 1-1.5cm long, pointed.

Flowering season: May-Jun

Habitat: Rocky outcrops, dry grassland, open woods; on calcareous soils

Distribution: Europe, N to S Sweden; Turkey. Only a garden plant in British Isles.

2 Lily-of-the-valley* ☠ ❀ ☒ *Convallaria majalis*

(Lily Family)

Hairless plant to 30cm tall. Lower leaves scale-like. 2 upper leaves broadly lanceolate and 10-20cm long, with parallel veins. Inflorescence one-sided and long-stalked. Bracts very small and shorter than flower stalk. Flowers nodding and bell-shaped, 5-7mm long. 6 perianth segments, fused together with small outwardly-directed tips. 6 stamens. Ovary superior. Fruit a red berry.

Flowering season: May-Jun

Habitat: Deciduous woods, scrub

Distribution: Most of Europe (in the S only in the mountains) eastwards to C Asia. In Britain native in calcareous woodland, but grown in gardens and often naturalized.

3 May Lily* ☠ ☒ *Maianthemum bifolium*

(Lily Family)

Plant to 20cm tall. Upper stem with fine, bristly hairs and usually 2 short-stalked heart-shaped leaves. Inflorescence a many-flowered raceme. Flowers in the axils of the scale-like bracts. Perianth segments 4, oval, to 3mm long and bending backwards. 6 stamens. Ovary superior. Fruit a yellow or red berry.

Flowering season: May-Jun

Habitat: Deciduous and coniferous woods. Avoids calcareous soils

Distribution: Much of Europe, east to Japan. Rare and local in Britain (E England only).

Note on Biology: The young plants produce only a single leaf in the first year, without flowering. After the first flower the plant continues to grow from a bud in the axil of an underground bract. The flowers are sweet-smelling and contain nectar. They are mainly pollinated by flies.

1|2
3

1

Common Solomon's-seal* ☠ ❀

(Lily Family) *Polygonatum multiflorum*

Plant to 50cm tall with leafy, rounded or weakly angled stem. Leaves alternate, ovate, to 15cm long. Flowers unscented, in short-stalked clusters of between 2 and 5, drooping from leaf axils and each up to 2cm long. Perianth segments fused over much of their length, and greenish towards the free tips. Flower tube somewhat pinched in the middle. Anthers hairy. 6 stamens joined in the bottom half of the flower to the flower tube. Ovary superior. Fruit a dark blue berry about 1cm across.
Flowering season: May-Jun
Habitat: deciduous woods, tall-herb communities; calcareous soils
Distribution: most of Europe; Turkey.
Similar species: Angular Solomon's-seal*, *P. odoratum.* This has a sharply-angled stem and nearly always solitary flowers. Stamens hairless. On rocky outcrops, dry grassland and open woods.
Whorled Solomon's-seal*☒, *P. verticillatum,* also has an angled stem. This species has lanceolate to linear upper stem leaves, mostly in whorls of 3. Flowers in groups of 1-7 with smaller, almost cylindrical tubes. Rare in Britain (Scotland only).
Note: The common Garden Solomon's-seal is a hybrid between *P. multiflorum* and *P. odoratum.*

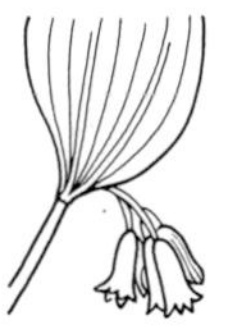

PART OF STEM
Common Solomon's-seal

PART OF STEM
Angular Solomon's-seal

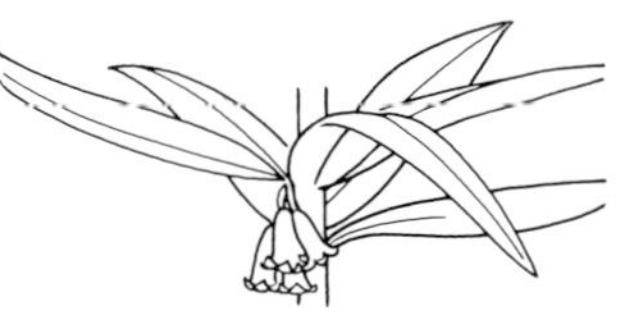

PART OF STEM
Whorled Solomon's-seal

2

Ramsons*

Allium ursinum

(Lily Family)

Plant to about 50cm tall, usually growing in large colonies. Leaves all basal, usually 2, to 20cm long, broadly lanceolate, pointed and long-stalked. Inflorescence clustered, at first encased in papery bracts which soon fall away. Flowers noticeably stalked. 6 perianth segments 8-12cm long, spreading. 6 stamens. Ovary superior.
Flowering season: Apr-Jun
Habitat: deciduous woodland, hedges
Distribution: much of Europe, E to the Caucasus. Abundant in British Isles.
Note on Biology: many species of the genus *Allium* contain strongsmelling and sharp tasting oils in all parts of the plant. The value of these compounds to the plants is not known for certain but is probably helps protect them from being eaten by animals. Many species have been cultivated as vegetables or spices. Examples are Onion *A. cepa,* Garlic *A. sativum,* Chives *A. schoenoprasum,* Welsh Onion *A. fistulosum,* Leek *A. ampeloprasum* and others. Ramsons, along with Garlic, is one of the most strongly smelling of all *Allium* species and was previously used in a similar way.

1

2

1

Spring Snowflake* ✿ ☒

Leucojum vernum

(Daffodil Family)

Hairless plant to 30cm tall with grass-like fleshy leaves. Flowers mostly solitary. Perianth segments 2-2.5cm long, all about the same length, with a green tip. 6 stamens. Ovary inferior.
Flowering season: Feb-Apr
Habitat: Deciduous woods, meadows
Distribution: much of Europe. Rare, and doubtfully native, in England.

2

Snowdrop* ✿ ☒

Galanthus nivalis

(Daffodil Family)

Hairless plant to 20cm tall with grass-like, fleshy leaves. Flowers solitary. Outer perianth segments oval, 15-20mm long, inner ones half as long, with a green spot at the edge. 6 stamens. Ovary inferior.
Flowering season: Feb-Mar
Habitat: Wet woodland, damp deciduous woods, scrub, meadows
Distribution: S Europe. In Britain mostly naturalized, although possibly native in SW England and Welsh borders.

3

Bog Arum ☠ ✿ ☒

Calla palustris

(Arum Family)

Plant to 40cm tall with stalked leaves about 12cm wide. Inflorescence Arumlike and enclosed in spathe, 2-4cm long. Ripe fruits red, berrylike.
Flowering season: May-Sep
Habitat: Marshes, wet woodland
Distribution: Much of Europe, east to Siberia and Japan; N America. In Britain naturalized in a few places.

4

Lesser Butterfly-orchid* ☒

Platanthera bifolia

(Orchid Family)

Hairless plant, to 50cm tall, with 2 large oval leaves towards base. Upper stem has only a few small leaves. Flowers white to cream. Lip strap-shaped, 6-10mm long. 2 inner segments forming a hood with upper outer segment. Anther lobes almost parallel. Spur thin and pointed.
Flowering season: May-Jul
Habitat: Open woods, meadows
Distribution: Europe; Asia.

5

Marsh Helleborine* ☒

Epipactis palustris

(Orchid Family)

Plant to 50cm tall with lanceolate leaves to 20cm long. 3 outer perianth segments lanceolate, 10-12mm long, brownish and somewhat spreading. 2 inner segments similar but white, often tinted pink at the base. Lip longer than other perianth segments. Lip has waist-like constriction and frilly edges. No spur.
Flowering season: Jun-Aug
Habitat: Marshes, fens
Distribution: most of Europe, except the high North; temperate parts of Asia.

1|2

3

4|5

1 Common Chickweed* *Stellaria media*

(Pink Family)

One of the commonest weeds. Very variable in petal-size, habit and other characters. Low-lying to erect, round-stemmed annual plant growing to 40cm tall. Stems with 1 or 2 rows of hairs, the line of hairs on each successive internode set at 90° further round stem. Leaves stalked, oval, pointed and hairless, stalks sometimes whiskered. Lower leaves almost unstalked. Flowers 5-partite, in the axils of the green bracts. Sepals 2-5mm long. Petals shorter than sepals, or more or less equally long, divided almost to their base. Stamens usually 3-8. 3 styles. Capsule opening with 6 teeth, measuring more than a third of capsule length.
Flowering season: Jan-Dec
Habitat: Fields, gardens, waste ground, footpaths, saltmarshes
Distribution: worldwide.

2 Greater Stitchwort* *Stellaria holostea*

(Pink Family)

One of our prettiest woodland and hedgerow spring flowers, growing to about 60cm. White flowers up to 3cm across, on slender stalks. Petals notched, and longer than the green sepals. Leaves narrow and stiff.
Flowering season: Apr-Jun
Habitat: Hedges, banks and wood margins
Distribution: Widespread in Europe. Common throughout most of Britain and Ireland, but rarer or absent in extreme N and W.

3 Thyme-leaved Sandwort* *Arenaria serpyllifolia*

(Pink Family)

Annual plant to 30cm tall, usually branched from the base. Stem with short backwardly-directed hairs, and often with glandular hairs as well. Leaves oval, pointed, 2-5mm long and hairy. Flowers 5-partite, in the axils of small bracts. Sepals 3-5 veined, somewhat hairy. Petals half to three quarters as long as sepals, undivided. Ovaries superior. 3 styles. Capsule oval, opening with six teeth measuring about a third of the capsule length.
Flowering season: May-Sep
Habitat: Open grassland, footpaths, fields, waste ground, walls
Distribution: Worldwide.
Note: Many of the white-flowered members of this family are very similar. They can be distinguished by characters of flower and fruit. The following is a brief overview:

Petals deeply divided into 2, (often almost to base):

- 3 styles, capsule opening with 6 teeth: genus *Stellaria* (see above)
- 5 styles, capsule opening with 10 teeth: genus *Cerastium* (see p 166)
- 5 styles, capsule opening with 5 teeth: genus *Myosoton*

Petals undivided, or notched in upper half only:

- 3 styles, capsule opening with 3 teeth: *Minuartia* (see p 166)
- 3 styles, capsule opening with 6 teeth, seeds with white appendages: *Moehringia*
- 3 styles, capsule opening with 6 teeth, seeds without appendages: *Arenaria* (see above)

1

2|3

1 Spring Sandwort* *Minuartia verna*

(Pink Family)

Cushion-forming plant growing to 15cm tall, with many flowering stems. Leaves linear, straight, mostly rather short, with 3 indistinct veins, hairless or with sparse glandular hairs. Stem leaves shorter than internodes. Flowers solitary or in loose clusters. Flower stalk usually longer than calyx and mostly with glandular hairs. Petals broadly lanceolate and pointed, 2.5-4.5mm long, noticeably 3-veined. Petals elliptical, about as long as sepals or slightly longer. 3 styles. Fruit oval, about as long as calyx and opening with 3 teeth.

Flowering season: May-Aug

Habitat: Rocks, dry grassland, scree

Distribution: Most of Europe, particularly on the high ground. In Britain mainly N England and Wales. Also W Ireland.

CALYX & FRUIT

2 Field Mouse-ear* *Cerastium arvense*

(Pink Family)

To 30cm tall, but often lower and mat-forming. Stem relatively unbranched with both normal and glandular hairs. Leaves narrowly lanceolate, pointed, to 4cm long. Lower leaf axils have mostly non-flowering branches or groups of leaves. Flower bracts small, oval with obvious margins. Flowers long-stalked, 5-partite. Sepals 7-10mm long, hairy. Petals 1-1.5cm long deeply divided at the tip. 5 styles. Fruit cylindrical, to twice as long as calyx, and opening with 10 teeth.

Flowering season: Apr-Jul

Habitat: Footpaths, dry grassland, walls; mostly on calcareous soils

Distribution: Europe; large parts of Asia and N Africa. In Britain mainly in the E.

CALYX & FRUIT

3 Sea Sandwort* *Honkenya peploides*

(Pink Family)

Hairless plant to about 30cm long, but low-growing, with creeping, fleshy stems rooting at the nodes. Leaves oval, thick, fleshy and pointed, clustered closely on the stems in groups of 4. Flowers solitary in the leaf axils or grouped at the end of the flowering stalks. Flower stalks 2-5mm long. Sepals 3-5mm long, oval and 1-veined. Petals undivided, white or greenish white, about the same length as sepals or shorter. 3 styles. Fruit round, opening with 3 teeth.

Flowering season: Jun-Jul

Habitat: Dunes and also in spray zone at the coast

Distribution: Coasts of W and N Europe and also N America.

CALYX & FRUIT

1
2
3

1 Corn Spurrey* *Spergula arvensis*

(Pink Family)

Annual plant, to 30cm tall, covered with glandular hairs. Leaves linear, with longitudinal furrows beneath, in whorls. White stipules present. Flowers 5-partite. Sepals oval, 2.5-4.5mm long. Petals rounded. 5 styles. Fruit opening with 5 teeth. Seeds blackish, 1-1.8mm across.
Flowering season: Jun-Oct. *Habitat:* Fields, footpaths, waste ground; avoids calcareous soils. *Distribution:* Worldwide.
The related Sea-spurreys°, *Spergularia,* are locally common, especially on the coasts of Britain and W Europe. They have opposite (not whorled) leaves and pinkish flowers, with 3 (not 5) styles.

2 Nottingham Catchfly* ☒ *Silene nutans*

(Pink Family)

Hairy plant to 50cm tall. Upper stem sticky. Lower leaves spoon-shaped, upper leaves lanceolate. Inflorescence bending over to one side with nodding flowers. Calyx tube-shaped with glandular hairs and 7-15mm long. Petals deeply 2-lobed, white above, often greenish beneath. 2-lobed scale in flowerthroat. 3 styles.
Flowering season: Jun-Sep. *Habitat:* Dry grassland, open woods, rocky outcrops *Distribution:* Most of Europe; Caucasus; Siberia. Local in England and Wales

3 Bladder Campion* *Silene vulgaris*

(Pink Family)

Plant to 60cm tall, usually hairless. Upper stem not sticky. Leaves oval to lanceolate and opposite. Flowers in loose inflorescences. Calyx inflated, pale green to whitish pink and with 20 veins. Petals deeply 2-lobed, white (occasionally pink). 3 styles.
Flowering season: May-Sep. *Habitat:* Meadows, tall-herb communities, open woods, footpaths *Distribution:* Europe; Asia; N Africa; N America. Common in Britain; local in Ireland.
Similar species: Sea Campion°, *S. uniflora* (*S. maritima*), is a mat-forming plant of coastal shingle (and lakes and mountains). It has larger, often solitary flowers. Often regarded as a subspecies of Bladder Campion.

4 White Campion* *Silene alba*

(Pink Family)

A pretty species, growing to about 1m. The leaves are oval or lanceolate, stalked lower down the plant and unstalked towards the top. The 5 white petals are 2-lobed. The white flowers (to about 30mm across) are fully open in the evenings, and attract moths as pollinators. Male and female flowers are on different plants. Where this species grows close to Red Campion (see p. 106), hybrid plants with pink flowers are sometimes found.
Flowering season: May-Oct. *Habitat:* Waste ground, rough field margins, hedgerows *Distribution:* Widespread in Europe, common in most of lowland Britain. Rare in Ireland, Wales, SW England and highland Scotland.
Similar species: Bladder and Sea Campion also have white flowers, but in both the calyx is much more inflated.

1|2
3
4

1 White Water-lily* ❀ ☒ *Nymphaea alba*

(Water-lily Family)

Water plant with thick, creeping rootstock and long-stalked floating leaves. Leaves large and round, more than 10cm across, reddish on the underside and green above, deeply split almost to halfway and with 15-20 curved lateral veins, joined towards tip. Flowers floating, large, up to 20cm in diameter, rounded towards the base and scented. 4 long sepals, white above and green below, falling quickly after the flower opens. Up to 30 long petals, white in colour, the outer ones somewhat longer than calyx. Sepals many, up to more than 100, outer ones often resembling petals. Ovary spherical. Stigma with 15-20 stigmatic surfaces, scarcely narrower than the fruit. Fruit oval, to 5cm long, at first on water surface, but ripening beneath the surface.

Flowering season: May-Aug

Habitat: Still or slowflowing water to about 3m deep

Distribution: Most of Europe, sometimes planted.

Note: When not in flower can be confused with Yellow Water-lily°, *Nuphar lutea* (see p. 36). However, in the latter species the floating leaves are green underneath, the lateral veins are not joined and there are wavy submerged leaves with a thin texture.

2 Christmas Rose ☠ ❀ ☒ *Helleborus niger*

(Buttercup Family)

Hairless plant to 30cm tall with upright stems. Upper leaves 1-3 and scalelike. Basal leaves with 7-9 lobes, shiny green, long-stalked and overwintering. Lobes narrowly lanceolate, with toothed margins towards the tip and widest in the first third. Flowers solitary, to 10cm across, with broadly ovate perianth segments, white or soft pink in colour, becoming greenish or red. Nectaries small, yellow or greenish. Stamens numerous, yellow. Fruit to 3cm long and beaked.

Flowering season: Sep-Jul

Habitat: Mountain woods and meadows. Only on calcareous soils

Distribution: Alps, Carpathians and Apennines. Commonly cultivated in Britain, but not naturalized.

Note on Biology: Usually flowers in late winter, the flowers growing up through the snow. Although few pollinating insects are active in this season, the stigmas remain receptive for a long period and are self-pollinated.

1
2

1 Wood Anemone* ❀ *Anemone nemorosa*

(Buttercup Family)

Mainly hairless plant growing to 30cm tall. Basal leaves not present at flowering time. 3 stem leaves in the upper part of the stem, long stalked and deeply-divided into 3 lobes. Flowers solitary, 2-4cm across. Perianth segments 6-8, sometimes even 12, white, often pink on the outside. Anthers yellow. Fruit small, rounded, and densely hairy.

Flowering season: Mar-May

Habitat: Mixed deciduous woods, hedges, shady meadows; on damp calcareous soils

Distribution: Most of Europe. Throughout British Isles, but rare in S Ireland.

2 White Buttercup ❀ *Ranunculus aconitifolius*

(Buttercup Family)

Hairless plant to 1m tall, with stalked basal leaves. Stem leaves unstalked, 3-7 lobed, with irregularly toothed margins. Flowers 1-2.5cm across. Flower-stalks hairy. Sepals falling off early. 5 white petals. Fruit small, with twisted beak.

Flowering season: May-Aug

Habitat: Damp meadows, woodland edges, stream-sides

Distribution: Mountains of C and S Europe.

3 River Water-crowfoot* *Ranunculus fluitans*

(Buttercup Family)

Water plant up to 5m long. Leaves many, fan-shaped, with long tips. Flowers floating, 1.5-3cm across. Petals obovate. Fruit small and oval.

Flowering season: Jun-Aug

Habitat: Streams and rivers

Distribution: W and C Europe, but absent from most of Scandinavia. Local in Britain, but rare in Wales. Rare in Ireland.

4 Baneberry* *Actaea spicata*

(Buttercup Family)

Hairless plant growing to 70cm tall. Leaves 3-lobed, with simple, or twice-divided, stalked leaflets and toothed margins. Flowers small, in dense, stalked clusters. Petals 7-12, outer ones 2-3mm long, inner ones shorter. Fruit a black berry.

Flowering season: Jun-Aug

Habitat: Shady woods, limestone pavement

Distribution: Most of Europe. In Britain very local in N England.

5 Garlic Mustard, Jack-by-the-hedge* *Alliaria petiolata*

(Cabbage Family)

Hairless plant growing to 90cm tall and smelling of garlic when crushed. Leaves stalked, heart-shaped and bluntly toothed. Flowers in a leafless cluster, short-stalked. 4 sepals, half as long as the white petals, (latter 46mm). Fruit a 1.5-2.5mm thick siliqua, 2-7cm long.

Flowering season: Apr-Jul

Habitat: Damp deciduous woods and scrub, hedgerows

Distribution: Europe; W Asia; common throughout much of British Isles.

1

2|3

4|5

1 Common Whitlowgrass* *Erophila verna*

(Cabbage Family)

Annual plant to 10cm tall, with stellate hairs. Rosette of long, somewhat toothed basal leaves. Flowers in a leafless, stalked cluster. Petals 4, small, 2-3mm long and divided to the middle. Fruit a silicula, 5-12mm long.
Flowering season: Mar-May
Habitat: Sandy fields, footpaths, walls
Distribution: Throughout Europe, but absent from most of Scandinavia; Asia.

2 Common Scurvygrass* *Cochlearia officinalis*

(Cabbage Family)

Very variable plant growing to about 50cm tall. Upper stem leaves unstalked, basal leaves heart-shaped. Flowers 8-10mm across; petals 4, white. Fruit a swollen silicula, longer than its stalk.
Flowering season: Apr-Sep
Habitat: Saltmarshes, cliffs and walls
Distribution: Throughout NW Europe; mainly coastal.
Similar species: Alpine Scurvygrass°☒, *C. pyrenaica* (plate) has smaller basal leaves, smaller flowers, and the fruit is shorter than its stalk. An inland species of mountains and rocky sites. Often treated as a subspecies of Common Scurvygrass.
Danish Scurvygrass°, *C. danica,* is a low-growing annual, with ivy-shaped lower leaves, stalked stem leaves and small, white or pale mauve flowers. Coastal, N and W Europe.

3 Water-cress* *Nasturtium officinale*

(Cabbage Family)

Virtually hairless plant growing to 50cm tall. Leaves divided into 3-9 leaflets. Flowers in a short leafless cluster. Sepals 2-3mm long, hairless. 4 petals, 3.5-5mm long. Fruit a siliqua, 13-18mm long and 1.8-2.5mm broad, in which the seeds are arranged in two rows.
Flowering season: Jun-Sep
Habitat: Streams, flushes, ditches
Distribution: Worldwide.
Note: Sometimes cultivated as a salad plant.
Similar species: Narrow-fruited Water-cress°, *N. microphyllum* . This has a capsule 16-24mm long and 1.2-1.8mm thick, with seeds in a single row.

4 Hoary Cress* *Cardaria draba*

(Cabbage Family)

Hairy plant to 60cm tall. Stem leaves unstalked and toothed, with basal tips encircling stem. Flowers densely clustered. Sepals 1.5-2mm long. 4 petals, 3-4mm long. Fruitstalks 3-4 times as long as fruit. Fruit 3-4.5mm long, heartshaped, 1-2 seeded, indehiscent (not splitting).
Flowering season: May-Jul
Habitat: Footpaths, wasteground
Distribution: S Europe; spread almost throughout the world. Common in S England.

1

2

3|4

1 Field Penny-cress* *Thlaspi arvense*

(Cabbage Family)

Annual, hairless plant to 40cm tall, with an upright, simple or branched stem. Leaves narrow, oval, entire or toothed. Lower leaves stalked, upper leaves unstalked and encircling stem at base. Inflorescence a loose, leafless raceme. Sepals 0.5-2mm long. 4 petals, 3-4mm long. Style 0.2mm long. Fruits 10-18mm long, rounded and flattened, divided at the tip, and with a 3-5mm broad wing around the edge.

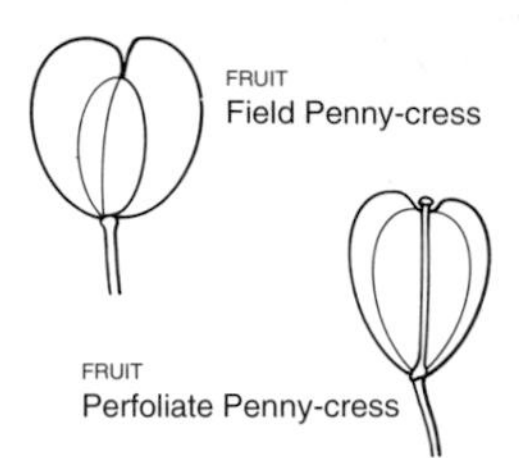

Flowering season: Apr-Sep

Habitat: Weed of arable land and waste places

Distribution: Virtually worldwide.

Similar species: Perfoliate Penny-cress°☒, *T. perfoliatum*. This has smaller flowers with petals 2-2.5mm long. Wing on the fruit only 1mm wide. Dry meadows, walls. Rare in Britain.

2 Hairy Rock-cress* *Arabis hirsuta*

(Cabbage Family)

Plant to 60cm tall, covered in erect hairs, both simple and branched. Stem leaves unstalked, toothed, growing close to each other and pressed to the stem. Bases of leaves rounded or encircling part of stem. Flowers in a dense, leafless cluster. Sepals 2-3.5mm long. 4 narrow petals, 4-7mm long. Fruit a 2-5cm long siliqua, closely appressed to the stem.

Flowering season: May-Jun

Habitat: Poor meadows, scrub

Distribution: Most of Europe; North Asia.

3 Shepherd's-purse* *Capsella bursa-pastoris*

(Cabbage Family)

Very variable, sparsely hairy annual plant growing to 40cm. Basal leaves in a rosette, stalked, mostly pinnate. Stem leaves encircling stem at base, with 2 pointed lobes. Upper stem leaves simple. Flowers in loose leafless cluster. Stamens 1-2mm long. Petals 4, 2-3mm long. Fruit stalked, inverted heart-shaped, with straight edges.

Flowering season: Mar-Dec

Habitat: Crops, paths, gardens, waste ground

Distribution: Virtually worldwide.

1|2
3

1 Thick-leaved Stonecrop* *Sedum dasyphyllum*

(Stonecrop Family)

Much-branched plant with glandular hairs, growing to 15cm tall. Leaves oval, thick, 5-7mm long, unstalked. Inflorescence umbel-like, loose and few-flowered. Flowers with 5-7 sepals, 1.5mm long, and 5-7 pointed petals, 3-4.5mm long. Petals pink to whitish, with red central stripe.
Flowering season: Jul-Aug
Habitat: Dry, sunny, rocky places
Distribution: S and W Europe. Introduced in S and C England. Also local (possibly native) in SW Ireland.

2 White Stonecrop* ❀ *Sedum album*

(Stonecrop Family)

Much-branched, hairless plant growing to 20cm tall. Leaves linear to cylindrical, 5-15mm, rounded in cross-section, often reddish, and 3-6mm across, unstalked. Inflorescence a many-flowered umbel-like cluster (corymb). Flowers mostly 5-partite. Sepals 1.2-1.5mm long. Petals 4-5mm long.
Flowering season: May-Aug
Habitat: Rocks, walls, dry grassland
Distribution: S and C Europe. Probably not native in British Isles.
Similar species: English Stonecrop°, *S. anglicum,* is much commoner in British Isles and undoubtedly native. It is smaller than White Stonecrop, with less-branched inflorescences.

3 Meadow Saxifrage* *Saxifraga granulata*

(Saxifrage Family)

Hairy plant to 50cm tall. Basal leaves in rosette, with bulbils in the leaf axils. Leaves kidney-shaped and long-stalked. Stem leaves short-stalked, lacking bulbils. Inflorescence a loose panicle, with glandular hairs. Sepals 3-5mm long. Petals narrow, oval 15mm long, white, yellow towards the base.
Flowering season: May-Jul
Habitat: Grassland, dry slopes, walls
Distribution: Most of Europe.
Similar species: Rue-leaved Saxifrage°, *S. tridactylites.* A much smaller plant, to 10cm tall, glandular, with spoon-shaped 3-lobed leaves and flowers 4mm long. Dry, sandy sites and old walls.

4 Livelong Saxifrage ❀ ☒ *Saxifraga paniculata*

(Saxifrage Family)

Densely carpeting plant up to 40cm tall, with many rosettes of leaves. Leaves narrowly spoon-shaped, toothed and producing a chalky exudate. Stem with few small leaves. Inflorescence a panicle. Sepals 1.5-2.5mm long. Petals 4-6mm long, oval or rounded, white and often with a red spot.
Flowering season: Jul-Aug
Habitat: Stony grassland, rocks
Distribution: C and E Europe; Turkey. Only a garden plant in British Isles.

1
2|3
4

1 Meadowsweet* *Filipendula ulmaria*

(Rose Family)

Plant to 2m tall, branched towards the top. Stem leaves dark green above, hairless, mostly with white felty hairs underneath. Leaves pinnate, with 5-11 fine-toothed leaflets. Flowers thickly clustered in a much-branched inflorescence. Sepals 1mm long. Petals 5 or 6, rounded to oval, 2-5mm long and yellowish-white in colour. Achenes smooth and twisted together in a spiral.

Flowering season: Jun-Aug

Habitat: Tall-herb communities, hay meadows, river banks

Distribution: Most of Europe, east to E Asia. Throughout British Isles.

Similar species: Dropwort°, F. vulgaris. Leaves green on both sides, divided, with 21-81 roughly-toothed leaflets. 6 petals, 5-10mm long. Achenes hairy, straight and erect. Dry grassland. Local on chalk and limestone in British Isles.

ACHENE
Meadowsweet

ACHENE
Dropwort

2 Wood Avens* *Geum urbanum*

(Rose Family)

Also known as Herb Bennet. A rather straggly plant to 60cm tall, with hairy stems and pinnate leaves. The open, erect, yellow flowers look a bit like those of the cinquefoils, but are rather small and inconspicuous. These turn into tight, slightly prickly fruit-heads.

Flowering season: Jun-Aug

Habitat: Scrub, hedges

Distribution: Throughout. Absent from N Scotland and Scottish Highlands.

3 Water Avens* *Geum rivale*

(Rose Family)

Plant to 70cm tall with pinnate leaves. Lower leaves with large, mainly 3-lobed terminal leaflets. Stem leaves mainly 3-lobed with rough-toothed leaflets and large stipules. Inflorescence many-flowered. Flowers long-stalked and nodding, becoming erect again in fruit. Sepals lanceolate, reddish-brown, 8-15mm long. Petals inverted heart-shaped, yellowish-white, scarcely longer than sepals. Fruit is a head of small achenes, topped by the hooked remains of the style.

Flowering season: May-Aug

Habitat: Damp meadows, streamsides, wet woods

Distribution: Europe; N Asia; N America. Locally common in Britain, but rare in SE England. Local in Ireland.

Note: These two species of *Geum* commonly produce hybrids where they meet. Hybrids show a range of intermediate forms.

1

2|3

1 Wild Strawberry* *Fragaria vesca*

(Rose Family)

Hairy plant to 20cm tall, with long, rooting runners. Leaves basal and long-stalked, 3-lobed, with roughly-toothed leaflets. The terminal tooth of the leaflet is longer than those on either side. Inflorescence with up to 5 flowers. Flower stalks with appressed or erect hairs. Flowers white, 1-1.5cm across, with 5 white petals which are touching or even slightly overlapping. The ripe fruit is a red, fleshy head in which the achenes are embedded.

Flowering season: May-Jun

Habitat: Open woods, woodland edges, scrub

Distribution: Most of Europe; N Asia.

Similar species: Hautbois Strawberry, *F. moschata,* has an 8-15 flowered inflorescence, leafstalk with erect hairs, and flowers 1.5-2.5cm across. Mainly C Europe. Introduced further N, including Britain.

2 Barren Strawberry* *Potentilla sterilis*

(Rose Family)

Hairy plant to 15cm tall with long, rooting runners. Leaves basal, long-stalked and 3-lobed, with toothed leaflets. The end tooth of the leaflet is noticeably smaller and shorter than the 2 neighbouring teeth. Inflorescence 1-3 flowered. Flowerstalk with erect hairs. Flowers white, 1-1.5cm across with 5 separated petals. Fruit not becoming fleshy when ripe.

Flowering season: Apr-May

Habitat: Mixed deciduous woods, woodland edges, footpaths

Distribution: Most of Europe, except Mediterranean area. Not in N Scotland.

3 White Cinquefoil ✿ *Potentilla alba*

(Rose Family)

Plant to 20cm tall, with silky, appressed hairs. Leaves basal, long-stalked and palmate, with 5 lanceolate leaflets with small teeth towards the tip. Leaves dark green and hairless above, covered in silvery hairs below. Stem curving upright, 1-2 flowered. Flowers white, 1.5-2.5cm across with 5 heart-shaped overlapping petals.

Flowering season: Apr-Jun

Habitat: Dry mixed deciduous woodland

Distribution: E and C Europe. Not native in British Isles or the rest of NW Europe.

Note: The genera *Fragaria* and *Potentilla* are similar, but species of the former can be distinguished by their fleshy, edible fruits. Both genera have 5 sepals and 5 epicalyx lobes.

1
2
3

1

Mountain Clover

Trifolium montanum

(Pea Family)

To 50cm tall, with appressed hairs. Leaves long-stalked with 3 lanceolate, finely-toothed leaflets. Flower heads terminal, rounded to oval, many-flowered, 1-2cm long. Calyx tube 10-veined with 5 narrow lobes. Corolla white, 7-10mm long.
Flowering season: May-Sep
Habitat: Meadows, open woods
Distribution: Especially C and SE Europe; W Asia. Not in British Isles.

2

White Clover*

Trifolium repens

(Pea Family)

Creeping plant rooting at the nodes. Leaf-stalks long. Leaves 3-lobed with obovate, finely-toothed leaflets, often white-banded. Flowers smelling faintly of honey. Flower heads in long stalked rounded clusters. Calyx tube 10-veined. Corolla white, 7-12mm long. Fruit enclosed in calyx and corolla.
Flowering season: May-Sep
Habitat: hay meadows, lawns, footpaths, waste ground
Distribution: Virtually worldwide.
Similar species: Alsike Clover°, *T. hybridum,* has an erect stem, is not creeping, and has a 5-veined calyx tube. Leaflets without pale band. Flowers purple or white, turning pink or brown. Meadows and footpaths.

3

Hairy Tare*

Vicia hirsuta

(Pea Family)

Slender, brittle, hairy annual plant growing to 50cm tall. Leaves pinnate, with simple or branched tendrils and 12-20 leaflets. Inflorescence stalked and 3-5 flowered. Inflorescence stalk with an awn-like projection 1-3mm long at the tip. Calyx 2-3mm long, teeth twice as long as tube. Corolla 3-4mm long. Fruit a hairy 2-seeded pod, 6-11mm long.
Flowering season: May-Aug
Habitat: Dry grassland, fields, waste ground.
Distribution: Europe; W Asia. Britain and Ireland.
Similar species: Smooth Tare°, *V. tetrasperma,* has leaves with 6-8 leaflets and lacks the projection on flower stalk. Flowers in 1s and 2s, calyx teeth shorter than tube, pod hairless and 4-seeded. Fields and grassland. S Scandinavia, C and S Europe. Britain, but absent from much of Scotland. Absent from Ireland.

4

Fairy Flax*

Linum catharticum

(Flax Family)

Delicate hairless annual plant, to 30cm tall. Leaves opposite, elliptical, unstalked, to 1cm long. Inflorescence a loose panicle. Flowers drooping in bud, later erect. Sepals 2-3mm long, pointed. 5 petals, 3-6mm long, white with yellow base.
Flowering season: Jul-Aug
Habitat: Dry and wet grassland; usually on calcareous soils
Distribution: Throughout Europe, except the N; in the S only in the mountains; W Asia.

1

2

3|4

1

Wood Sorrel* ☠ *Oxalis acetosella*

(Wood Sorrel Family)

Weakly hairy plant to 12cm tall, with clover-like leaves. Leaves basal, stalked, with 3 heart-shaped leaflets. Flowers long-stalked, basal, 5-partite. Sepals narrowly oval, 4-5mm long; petals 10-15mm long, white with pinkish veins.
Flowering season: Apr-May
Habitat: Shady woods
Distribution: Europe; Asia; N America.

2

White Rock-rose* ✿ ☒ *Helianthemum apenninum*

(Rock-rose Family)

Plant to 30cm tall, woody towards the base, and covered with felty hairs. Leaves about 3cm long, narrow and curled under towards the edges. 2 short, needle-like stipules at base of leaves. Inflorescence 3-10 flowered. Flowers 2-3cm across with 3 short outer and 5 longer inner sepals. Petals 5 and rounded. Stamens numerous.
Flowering season: May-Jul
Habitat: Dry grassland, rocks; on calcareous soils
Distribution: S and W Europe; rare in SW England.

3

White Bryony* ☠ *Bryonia dioica*

(Cucumber Family)

Climbing plant with rough stems up to 4m long. Leaves short stalked, 5-lobed and coarsely toothed. Dioecious. Flowers in clusters. Sepals 3-4mm long. Petals 5, greenish-white, rather funnel-shaped and fused, up to 1cm long. Fruit red.
Flowering season: Jun-Jul
Habitat: Hedges, woodland edges, waste ground
Distribution: W and C Europe. Common in lowland England; not native in Scotland and Ireland.

4

Enchanter's-nightshade* *Circaea lutetiana*

(Willowherb Family)

To about 60cm tall, covered with short hairs. Leaves opposite, stalked, oval and pointed. Inflorescence a leafless spike. Sepals 2, glandular. Petals 2, deeply divided and 2-4mm long. Fruit a nut about 3-4mm long, covered in hooked hairs.
Flowering season: Jul-Aug
Habitat: Mixed woodland, clearings
Distribution: Europe, N to S Scandinavia; Turkey; N Africa.

5

Spiked Water-milfoil* *Myriophyllum spicatum*

(Water-milfoil Family)

Water plant up to 3m long. Leaves pinnate in whorls of 4, with many feathery leaflets. Flowers also whorled, whitish, stalkless and 4-partite. Petals about 2mm long.
Flowering season: Jul-Sep
Habitat: Still water
Distribution: Worldwide. Locally common in British Isles.

1

2|3

4|5

1 Wild Carrot* — *Daucus carota*

(Carrot Family)

Stiffly hairy plant to 1m tall. Leaves stalked, 2- to 3-pinnate, with pinnatifid segments, and with enlarged sheath-like base encircling stem. Inflorescence a flat or curved umbel, surrounded at the base by an involucre of pinnate bracts. Flower stalks arching over towards centre in fruit. Sepals absent. 5 petals with heartshaped margins; largest towards edge of umbel. Central flower usually has red or purple corolla. Fruits with longitudinal rows of spines.

Flowering season: Jun-Oct

Habitat: Meadows, rough grassland; common in England on calcareous soils

Distribution: almost worldwide. Absent from far N of Europe.

2 Great Masterwort — *Astrantia major*

(Carrot Family)

Hairless plant to 1m tall. Stem with few leaves and usually branched only towards the tip. Basal leaves long-stalked, mostly 5-lobed. Lobes toothed and often slightly overlapping. Flowers inconspicuous, in simple umbels. Many involucral bracts, white to pink and up to twice as long as umbel rays and fruits.

Flowering season: Jun-Sep

Habitat: Meadows, scrub, woodland edges; mainly on chalky soils

Distribution: C and S Europe. Naturalized locally in W Britain.

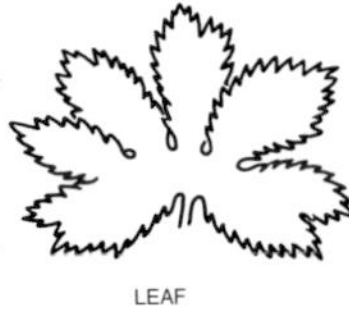

LEAF

3 Greater Burnet-saxifrage* — *Pimpinella major*

(Carrot Family)

Hairless plant to 1m tall with furrowed, ridged stem. Basal and stem leaves present. Base of stem leaves only slightly enlarged into a sheath. Leaves simply pinnate with unevenly toothed lobes. Inflorescence a double umbel. Involucre absent. Petals 1-1.5mm long. Style 1.5-2mm long and longer than the young fruit. Fruit oval, hairless.

Flowering season: Jun-Aug

Habitat: Rich meadows, tall-herb communities

Distribution: Most of Europe, except for far W and N. Locally common in E England and SW Ireland; elsewhere local and rare.

Similar species: Burnet-saxifrage°, *P. saxifraga*, has finely-ribbed stem, and mostly rounded leaf lobes. Style 0.8-1mm long. Fruit broadly oval to rounded. Dry grassland, heaths and open woodland.

PART OF LEAF Greater Burnet-saxifrage

PART OF LEAF Burnet-saxifage

1

2|3

1 Sanicle*

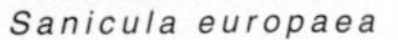
Sanicula europaea

(Carrot Family)

Plant to 50cm tall. Leaves basal, long-stalked and palmately 5-lobed, with rough, toothed margins. Stem leaves small, unstalked. Flowers arranged in small umbels, with the side branches generally in groups of 3. Flowers surrounded by 4-8 involucral bracts. Outer flowers male, many; inner flowers female, 1-3. Fruit rounded and spiny.

Flowering season: May-Jun

Habitat: Mixed deciduous woods, beech woods; calcareous soils.

Distribution: Europe, W Asia.

2 Cow Parsley, Queen Anne's Lace*

(Carrot Family) *Anthriscus sylvestris*

Almost hairless branched plant to 1.5m tall. Leaves 2 to 3 pinnate, dark green, somewhat shiny, with divided lobes. Flowers arranged in a double umbel. Involucre lacking. Bracteoles with several broadly lanceolate lobes. Petals to 2mm long. Fruit elongate, unribbed, black to dark brown and shiny when ripe.

FRUIT

Flowering season: May-Aug

Habitat: Roadsides, meadows, scrub, woodland margins

Distribution: whole of Europe; N Asia; N Africa.

3 Hairy Chervil

Chaerophyllum hirsutum

(Carrot Family)

Hairy plant to 1m tall with a branched stem, slightly thickened at the nodes. Leaves stalked, twice pinnate with roughly toothed lobes. Flowers in double umbels. Bracts absent. Bracteoles lanceolate and fringed with hairs. Petals with fringed margins. Fruit spindle-shaped, 8-12mm long, with longitudinal ridges.

Flowering season: May-Aug

Habitat: Rich meadows, streamsides

Distribution: European mountains. Very rare, and presumably introduced in NW England.

Similar species: Rough Chervil°, *C. temulentum*, is found in much of Europe including Britain and Ireland. It has purple-spotted, bristly stems.

FRUIT
Rough Chervil

4 Ground-elder*

Aegopodium podagraria

(Carrot Family)

Hairless plant to 1m tall, with thin, far-creeping rhizomes, white when young. Leaves once to twice-trifoliate, with finely-toothed lobes. Involucre and bracteoles absent. Petals 1.5mm long. Fruit oval with fan-like ridges.

Flowering season: Jun-Aug

Habitat: Wet woodland, hedges, gardens (a persistent garden weed in British Isles)

Distribution: Europe; N Asia.

1|2
3
4

1 Cowbane* ☠ *Cicuta virosa*

(Carrot Family)

Plant to 1.5m tall. Leaves twice or three times pinnate, with narrowly lanceolate, toothed and pointed lobes. Bracts absent. Bracteoles very narrow, pointed and reflexed. Flowers with pointed sepals. Petals 1mm long. Fruits rounded when ripe, 1.5mm long and about 2mm across. Calyx lobes of ripe fruit about 0.5mm long.

Flowering season: Jul-Aug

Habitat: Ditches, reed beds

Distribution: C and N Europe; N Asia. Rather local in British Isles.

2 Caraway* ✿ *Carum carvi*

(Carrot Family)

Hairless plant to 1m tall with stem often branched from base. Leaves 2- to 3-pinnate with narrow segments. Lower leaves stalked; upper leaves unstalked. Umbels irregular. Bracts and bracteoles usually absent. Flowers white or pinkish. Fruit long, elliptical, brown with pale ribs, aromatic when crushed.

Flowering season: May-Jul

Habitat: Hay meadows, pasture, footpaths; cultivated as herb

Distribution: Most of Europe; N Africa; Asia; N America. Rare in British Isles, mainly in SE England.

3 Wild Angelica* *Angelica sylvestris*

(Carrot Family)

Hairless plant to 2m tall. Leaves large, twice-pinnate, with elliptic, toothed lobes. Bracts usually absent. Bracteoles numerous. Petals to 15mm long, white or pink, at first greenish. Fruits oval with winged edges, 4-6mm long.

Flowering season: Jul-Aug

Habitat: Wet woods; damp meadows, tall-herb communities

Distribution: Europe; Siberia.

4 Hogweed* *Heracleum sphondylium*

(Carrot Family)

Bristly-hairy plant to 2m tall. Leaves large and divided, lower ones stalked. Stem leaves unstalked, with inflated sheaths. Bracts absent. Bracteoles numerous. Fruit oval, flat, with narrow, winged margin.

Flowering season: Jun-Sep

Habitat: Roadsides, hay meadows, banks, ditches, tall-herb communities

Distribution: most of Europe; common throughout British Isles.

FRUIT
Hogweed

1|2

3|4

1 Serrated Wintergreen* ☒ *Orthilia secunda*

(Wintergreen Family)

Plant to 20cm tall. Leaves limited to lower third of stem, broadly lanceolate and pointed, with finely-toothed edge and short stalks. Flowers in a dense one-sided raceme. Sepals small, triangular. Petals 3-4mm long, bell-shaped, whitish green. Anthers without appendages. Styles straight.
Flowering season: Jun-Jul
Habitat: Humus-rich pine woods
Distribution: most of Europe; N Asia; N America. In British Isles very local (S Wales, N England, Scotland, N and C Ireland).

2 One-flowered Wintergreen* ☒

(Wintergreen Family) *Moneses uniflora*

Plant to 15cm tall with leaves in a basal rosette. Leaves short-stalked, rounded and finely-toothed. Stem with a single terminal flower 12-25mm across. Sepals broad and oval, separated to base. Petals white, 8-12mm long, spreading. Anthers with 2 long, horn-like appendages. Style straight.
Flowering season: May-Jul
Habitat: Coniferous woods
Distribution: N and C Europe; N Asia; N America. In British Isles a rare species, confined to a few sites in Scotland.

3 Round-leaved Wintergreen* ☒

(Wintergreen Family) *Pyrola rotundifolia*

Plant to 40cm tall with leaves in a basal rosette. Leaves long-stalked, with round to broadly oval shaped blade with toothed margins. Flowers evenly distributed around stalk, in a short spike. Sepals 2-3 times as long as broad, pointed. Petals white, 6-8mm long, bell-shaped. Anthers with short horns. Style S-shaped, much longer than ovary, extending beyond petals and thickened below the stigma.
Flowering season: Jun-Aug
Habitat: Pine and larch woods; on calcareous soils
Distribution: Europe; N Asia; N America. Very local in Britain. Very rare in Ireland.
Similar species: Intermediate Wintergreen* ☒, *P. media,* resembles previous species but has a straight style.
Common Wintergreen* ☒, *P. minor,* has petals 3-5mm long, anthers lacking appendages, style straight, at most as long as ovary and not exceeding petal length, not thickened beneath stigma.

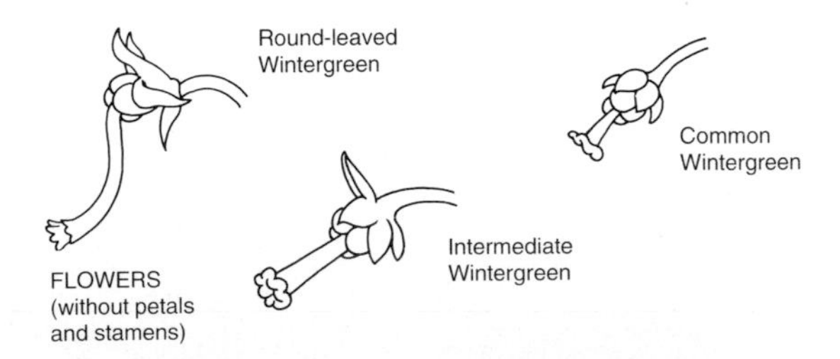

1
2|3

1 Labrador Tea*☠☒ *Ledum palustre*

(Heath Family)

Small evergreen shrub to 1.5m tall, with upright stems. Leaves linear-lanceolate to broadly lanceolate, leathery, with edges rolled downwards. Leaves hairless above and covered with reddish brown felty hairs beneath. Inflorescence a creamy white umbel with many flowers. Calyx 5-toothed with 5 rounded lobes. Corolla white, spreading, 10-15mm across with 5 obovate, separate petals. Fruit an oval 5-celled capsule, 3-6mm long.
Flowering season: May-Jun
Habitat: Bogs
Distribution: N Europe south to N Germany; N Asia; N America.
In Britain a rare plant of bogs in C Scotland where possibly native, and a rare escape elsewhere.
Note: This species has become rare over much of its range due to draining of raised bogs.
Note on Biology: The flowers give off a very strong scent which attracts insects, in such a concentration that small flies are sometimes even killed by it.

2 Bearberry*☒ *Arctostaphylos uva-ursi*

(Heath Family)

Low-growing many-branched dwarf shrub. Leaves evergreen, hard, obovate, 1-3cm long, entire, with pale hairy margins. Leafstalk 1mm long. Inflorescence 3-10 flowered. 5 sepals, hairless, fused. Corolla ovoid and fused, with 5 short lobes at the tip and hairy on the inside. Fruit a red berry.
Flowering season: May-Jul
Habitat: Pine woods, sandy areas, heath, heather moor
Distribution: Europe; N Asia; N America, local in N England, Scotland and Ireland.
Similar species: Cowberry°, *Vaccinium vitis-idaea,* has evergreen leaves with a thick downrolled margin and the corolla is hairless within. In British Isles mainly in N.
Bilberry°, *V. myrtillus,* has a winged stem. This is a deciduous species with flat, finely-toothed leaves and greenish flowers, sometimes shot with purple. Fruit a dark blue berry 5-8mm across. Heather moors, acid woods. Throughout British Isles, but rare in E Anglia and Midlands.
Bog Bilberry°, *V. uliginosum,* is another deciduous species. This has entire, blue-green thin leaves. Corolla short, 4-6mm long, white to pink. Fruit a dark blue berry 6-8mm across. Bogs and Heaths. Absent from Ireland. In Britain mainly in Scotland and N England.

FLOWER
Bearberry

FLOWER
Cowberry

FLOWER
Bog Bilberry

FLOWER
Bilberry

1
2

1 Bog-rosemary* ❀ *Andromeda polifolia*

(Heath Family)

Hairless plant to 30cm tall. Stems creeping, often amongst bog-mosses. Leaves evergreen, narrowly lanceolate, 1-5cm long with rolled back margins. Flowers in groups of 2-5. Calyx 5-lobed. Corolla white or pale pink, fused, ovoid, 5-8mm long with 5 short lobes. 10 stamens.

Flowering season: May-Jun

Habitat: Bogs and wet heaths

Distribution: Europe, except Mediterranean; N America: N Asia. In Britain mainly in mid-Wales, N England and S Scotland. C Ireland.

2 Chickweed Wintergreen* ☒ *Trientalis europaea*

(Primrose Family)

Hairless plant to 25cm tall. Lower and middle stem leaves in threes and very small, remaining leaves at the stem tip in whorls of 5-12, lanceolate, 2-5cm long. Flowers few and long-stalked, in the axils of the upper leaves. Calyx 4-6mm long. Corolla flat and open or somewhat funnel-shaped, divided almost to the base into 6 or 7 lobes and up to 15mm across.

Flowering season: May-Jul

Habitat: Wooded bogs, spruce woods

Distribution: N and C Europe; Asia; N America. In Britain mainly in Scotland and NE England. Absent from Wales and Ireland.

3 Bogbean* ❀ ☒ *Menyanthes trifoliata*

(Bogbean Family)

Hairless plant to 35cm tall. Leaves at the tips of subterranean creeping stems, long-stalked at the base and widening into a sheath. Leaf-blade trifoliate, with ovate leaflets. Inflorescence an erect condensed raceme, on a leafless stalk. Calyx split almost to the base into 5 lobes. Corolla pinkish-white, with short funnel-shaped tube and 5 hairy, spreading or reflexed lobes.

Flowering season: May-Jun

Habitat: Fens, wet places, reed beds

Distribution: Europe; Asia; N America.

4 Swallow-wort, Vincetoxicum ☠

(Milkweed Family) *Vincetoxicum hirundinaria*

Sparsely hairy plant to 1m tall with unbranched stem. Leaves opposite, short-stalked, broadly lanceolate with rounded or heartshaped base. Underside of leaves with short hairs along veins. Flowers in the upper leaf axils surrounded by small lanceolate bracts. Calyx lobes 2mm long, pointed. Corolla funnel-shaped, 4-7mm wide and deeply 5-lobed. Fruit a long pod to 7cm long. Seeds 6-7mm long, narrowly oval and flat, with white hairs at the tip.

Flowering season: May-Aug

Habitat: Dry grassland, open woods, scrub

Distribution: Europe except the N and NW; Asia; N Africa. Absent from British Isles.

1

2

3|4

1 Common Comfrey* *Symphytum officinale*

(Borage Family)

Thickly hairy plant to 1.5m tall. Stem angled and winged, unbranched or branched only towards the top. Leaves lanceolate, lower ones stalked and up to 25cm long, the upper ones shorter and unstalked. The wings of the leaves project downwards along the stem as far as the next leaf. Inflorescences in axils of upper leaves, dense, hanging over to one side. Calyx 5-lobed almost to base. Corolla 1.2-2cm long, tube-shaped and fused, with 5 small scales in the throat between the 5 stamens. Style projecting beyond corolla.

Flowering season: May-Jul

Habitat: Damp meadows, river banks, fens

Distribution: Europe; Asia.

Note: This species has several colour varieties. The commonest form has purple or pinkish-violet flowers, and specimens with white or yellowish-white flowers are also quite common.

2 Hedge Bindweed* ❀ *Calystegia sepium*

(Bindweed Family)

Hairless plant, with annual, climbing stems 2-3m long. Leaves heartshaped or arrowshaped, pointed, stalked and alternate. Flowers solitary in the leaf axils, 3.5-4cm long, with 2 broad, lanceolate sepal-like bracts at the base, partly obscuring calyx. Calyx 10mm long. Corolla funnel-shaped, white.

Flowering season: Jun-Sep

Habitat: Wet woods, reed beds, hedges

Distribution: Worldwide.

Similar species: Large Bindweed* ❀, *C. sylvatica,* has inflated bracts at the base of the flower, overlapping each other and completely enclosing the calyx. Corolla to 7.5cm long. Forms may have either white or pink-striped flowers. A garden escape; native of SE Europe.

3 Black Nightshade* *Solanum nigrum*

(Nightshade Family)

Weakly hairy plant to 60cm tall with a round, smooth stem. Leaves oval to triangular, toothed and stalked. Inflorescences in the axils of the upper leaves, containing 4-10 flowers on a stalk, each 1.5-2.5cm long. Calyx with oval short teeth and pointed lobes. Corolla white, with deeply 5-lobed margin, 6-10mm across. Fruit a black berry.

Flowering season: Jun-Oct

Habitat: Waste ground, fields, gardens

Distribution: Worldwide. Lowland England and Wales, most common in the S and E.

Similar species: Hairy Nightshade, *S. luteum,* has an angled stem with a dense covering of hairs. Calyx teeth pointed. Fruit golden yellow to red. Not in British Isles, except as a casual.

FRUIT & CALYX
Black Nightshade

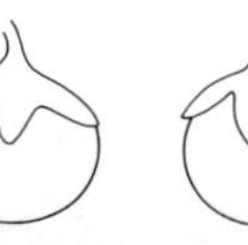

FRUIT & CALYX
Hairy Nightshade

1

2|3

1

White Horehound* ☒

Marrubium vulgare

(Mint Family)

Plant to 60cm tall, covered with dense felted hair. Leaves opposite, stalked, broadly oval, 2-4cm long, wrinkled and coarsely toothed at the margin. Flowers short-stalked in tight almost rounded whorls in the axils of the upper leaves. Calyx 4-6mm long with a thick covering of stellate hairs and with 10 spiny teeth, hooked when in fruit. Corolla 6-7mm long, 2-lipped, softly hairy, middle lobe of the lower lip three times as long as the side lobes. 4 stamens, enclosed in corolla tube.

Flowering season: Jun-Aug

Habitat: Footpaths, waste ground

Distribution: S and C Europe, N to S Sweden and S England (occasional); C Asia.

2

Gypsywort*

Lycopus europaeus

(Mint Family)

Almost hairless plant growing to 1m tall. Stem simple or branched. Leaves opposite, with short stalks or unstalked, lanceolate, 3-8cm long, coarsely toothed, hairless or sparsely hairy. Flowers unstalked, in many flowered whorls in the axils of the upper leaves. Calyx 2.5-4mm long, teeth with long points, and twice as long as tube. Corolla 4-6mm long with pure white upper lip and 3-lobed red-spotted lower lip. 2 stamens clearly protruding from flower.

Flowering season: Jul-Sep

Habitat: reed beds, ditches, overgrown pond margins

Distribution: Europe; Asia. In British Isles throughout lowlands, but more scattered in N Scotland and Ireland.

3

White Dead-nettle*

Lamium album

(Mint Family)

Sparsely hairy plant to 50cm tall with a rectangular, usually unbranched stem. Leaves opposite, stalked and rounded to lanceolate, heart-shaped or rounded at the base and often sharply pointed; roughly toothed at the margins. Flowers unstalked, in whorled clusters of the upper leaves. Calyx funnel-shaped with unequal pointed teeth. Corolla 2-2.5cm long, with arching upper lip and folded lower lip. Sides of the lower lip with 1 narrow lanceolate tooth. 4 stamens lying close under the upper lip, with brown and white bearded anthers.

Flowering season: Apr-Aug

Habitat: Scrub, footpaths, waste ground

Distribution: Most of Europe, except far N; Nand E Asia. Throughout British Isles, but rare or local in N and W and probably only introduced in Ireland

1|2

3

1 Eyebright* *Euphrasia*

(Figwort Family)

The eyebrights are a difficult group to identify. There are about 30 species in the region, but only expert botanists can distinguish them. They are small annuals (to about 40cm) with terminal flowers, clustered in a small spike. The flowers have a 4-toothed calyx, and the corolla has a large, 3-lobed lower lip and a smaller upper lip which is bent backwards. The flowers are usually white with a yellow throat and purplish lines.
All eyebrights are semi-parasites, getting their water and mineral supplies from the roots of their host plant (often grasses).
One of the commonest eyebrights in the British Isles is *E. nemorosa*, which has rather large flowers, but no glandular hairs.
Flowering season: Jun-Sep
Habitat: Grassland, heath, woodland edges
The species illustrated is another large-flowered eyebright, with glandular hairs, *E. rostkoviana*, which is widespread in Europe, and local in the British Isles.

2 Woodruff*☠ *Galium odoratum*

(Bedstraw Family)

Plant to 30cm tall, with leaves in whorls of 6-9, smelling of hay when dried. Leaves lanceolate and entire. Flowers clustered and terminal or in the axils of the upper leaves and with few flowers. Calyx lacking. Corolla 4-6mm wide, funnel-shaped with a 1mm long tube and 4 spreading lobes. Fruit nut-like and rounded, 2-3mm long, with hooked hairs.
Flowering season: Apr-May
Habitat: Woods, especially Beech.
Distribution: Most of Europe; N Asia.

3 Hedge-bedstraw* *Galium mollugo*

(Bedstraw Family)

Mostly hairless plant growing to about 1.5m tall. Stem upright, somewhat rectangular and thickened at the nodes. Leaves narrow and in whorls of 4-8, to 3cm long, pointed, entire and with a single vein. Flowers in panicles. Corolla to 4mm wide, white or cream in colour, the 4 petals spreading. Each petal with a narrow point at tip.
Flowering season: Jun-Oct
Habitat: Meadows, hedges, woodland margins
Distribution: Much of Europe, N to S Scandinavia. Common throughout England and S Scotland, occasional elsewhere in British Isles.

1

2|3

1

Spiked Rampion* ☒ *Phyteuma spicatum*

(Bellflower Family)

Plant to 70cm tall. Basal leaves heart-shaped, long-stalked, irregularly twice-toothed and often with dark markings. Upper stem leaves unmarked. Flowers in an oval to cylindrical head. Calyx with 5 linear lobes. Corolla white, rarely with a pale blue wash, cylindrical or tube-shaped. 5 corolla lobes joined at base and tip at first, later separating at tips. Ovary inferior. 2 stigmas. Fruit a rounded capsule, opening through 2 pores at the top.

Flowering season: May-Jul. *Habitat:* Deciduous woods, scrub, mountain meadows; on humus-rich damp soils. *Distribution:* C Europe, N to S Norway, and from the Pyrenees as far as C Russia. Very rare in S England.

2

Scented Mayweed* *Matricaria recutita*

(Daisy Family)

Hairless plant to 60cm tall with a much-branched stem. Leaves mostly twice-pinnate. Inflorescence to 2.5cm wide, with conical base. Ray florets white; tube florets yellow. Fruits weakly rectangular, grey-brown, with 4-5 pale, longitudinal ridges.

Flowering season: May-Jul. *Habitat:* Fields, footpaths, waste land; on loamy soils. Sometimes cultivated as a medicinal herb.

Distribution: Most of Europe. Virtually absent from Ireland. Mainly lowland England and Wales; rare in Scotland.

3

Daisy* *Bellis perennis*

(Daisy Family)

Low-growing plant, with flowering stems to 15cm tall. Leaves spoon-shaped, weakly toothed and stalked, growing in a basal rosette. Stem leafless and single-headed. Tube florets yellow; ray florets white or pink.

Flowering season: Jun-Sep. *Habitat:* Short grassland; common in garden lawns

Distribution: Europe; Turkey; widely naturalized.

4

Canadian Fleabane* *Erigeron canadensis*

(Daisy Family)

Somewhat hairy plant to 1m tall. Stem leaves lanceolate, entire or somewhat toothed. Flower heads numerous, each 3-5mm across. Ray florets only slightly longer than bracts and white in colour. Tube florets a little shorter and pale yellow. Fruits about 1mm long, hairy with yellowish pappus.

Flowering season: Jun-Oct. *Habitat:* Waste areas, footpaths, railway embankments.

Distribution: Worldwide. Introduced from N America. In Britain commonest in S and E.

5

Corn Chamomile* *Anthemis arvensis*

(Daisy Family)

Hairy plant to about 50cm tall, aromatic, but not unpleasantly so. Flower heads 2-3cm across. Leaves often woolly underneath.

Flowering season: Jun-Jul. *Habitat:* Arable land and waste ground, on lime-rich soils

Distribution: Throughout, except far N. In Britain mainly in S and E England, scattered in E Scotland. Absent from Ireland.

1|2

3

4|5

1

Feverfew*

Tanacetum parthenium

(Daisy Family)

Very aromatic plant with a characteristic smell, growing to about 60cm. Leaves are a light yellow-green. The flower heads each look rather like a Daisy, with a yellow centre, surrounded by a ring of short 'petals'.

Flowering season: Jul-Aug

Habitat: Waste ground, walls, old gardens, hedges, roadsides

Distribution: Throughout, N to S Sweden. Throughout British Isles, but rather scattered in N and W Scotland, and in Ireland.

Note: As you would expect from its name, Feverfew is an effective medicinal herb. It has been proved to help relieve migraine and other headaches, as well as arthritis and asthma.

2

Oxeye Daisy*

Leucanthemum vulgare

(Daisy Family)

Sparsely hairy plant to 1m tall. Basal leaves spoon-shaped, long-stalked and toothed at margins. Stem leaves long, entire or pinnate; upper leaves unstalked. Flower heads to 5cm across. Ray florets white, tube florets yellow.

Flowering season: May-Sep

Habitat: Meadows, open woods

Distribution: Most of Europe. Throughout British Isles, but less common in NW Scotland.

3

Scentless Mayweed*

Tripleurospermum inodorum

(Daisy Family)

To 80cm tall, much branched. Stem and leaves hairless, although somewhat hairy when young. Leaves alternate, irregularly 2-3 pinnate, with many narrow lobes. Flower heads 3-4.5cm across; receptacle domed. Ray florets white, up to 2cm long; tube florets yellow. Bracts with translucent, often dark brown rim. Fruits deeply furrowed with longitudinal ridges and rounded oil glands.

Flowering season: Jun-Oct

Habitat: Rich agricultural land, waste land, footpaths, dunes

Distribution: most of Europe.

4

Yarrow*

Achillea millefolium

(Daisy Family)

Hairy plant to 60cm tall with an erect stem, branching towards the top. Leaves 2-3 pinnate, with narrow lanceolate tips. Flower heads 4-8mm broad, forming a dense umbel-like panicle. Bracts 3-4.5mm long. Ray florets white or pinkish. Tube florets yellowish-white. Fruits 1.8-2mm long, with somewhat winged margins, without pappus.

Flowering season: Jun-Oct

Habitat: Rich meadows, pastures

Distribution: Europe; N Asia.

1|2
3|4

1

Rannoch Rush* ☒ *Scheuchzeria palustris*

(Rannoch Rush Family)

Hairless plant growing to 20cm tall with a leafy stem. Leaves grass-like, with a sheath broadening towards the base. Flowers in small clusters, each with 6 small, yellowish-green petals. Fruit is very distinctive, with 3 fused, somewhat inflated follicles.

Flowering season: May-Jul

Habitat: Raised bogs, blanket bogs

Distribution: N and C Europe; N Asia; N America. A very rare plant in Britain, extinct in several former localities and now found only on Rannoch Moor in Scotland.

2

Broad-leaved Pondweed* *Potamogeton natans*

(Pondweed Family).

Floating aquatic with stems up to 2m long. Leaves long-stalked, leathery and oval, heart-shaped or rounded at the base, and up to 10cm long. Flowers held up above the water in short spikes. Flowers small, with 4 stamens, each with a petal-like green appendage. Fruits greenish.

Flowering season: May-Aug

Habitat: Still or slow-flowing water

Distribution: Worldwide.

Note: There are many floating and submerged *Potamogeton* species. These are difficult to distinguish without the help of detailed Floras.

3

Sea Arrowgrass* *Triglochin maritima*

(Arrowgrass Family)

Hairless plant to 70cm, with grass-like leaves arising from a basal rosette. Leaves with a sheath-like base. Inflorescence a long-stalked, many-flowered dense spike. Flowerstalks very short. 6 perianth segments, 1.5-2mm long, yellowish-green. Carpels fused. 6 stigmas. Fruit oval, splitting into 6 when ripe.

Flowering season: Jun-Jul

Habitat: Coastal saltmarshes; also in inland salty areas

Distribution: Most of the Northern Hemisphere.

4

Common Duckweed* *Lemna minor*

(Duckweed Family)

Small water plant, not divided into stem and leaves. Plant leaf-like and oval, floating on the surface of the water, 2-6mm long. Has a single thread-like root extending into the water below. Flowers tiny and very rare.

Flowering season: Apr-Jul

Habitat: Still and slow-flowing water

Distribution: Worldwide. Common throughout British Isles, except extreme N.

Similar species: Greater Duckweed*, *Spirodela polyrhiza* is similar but is larger, with many spreading roots below (from 2-10). Ponds, ditches throughout Europe.

1|2
3
4

1

Herb-paris*☠ *Paris quadrifolia*

(Lily Family)

Hairless plant to 40cm tall with an erect stem. Leaves in a whorl at tip of stem, usually 4, sometimes 5 or 6. Leaf surface has a noticeable network of veins. Flowers terminal, on a 2-5cm stalk. Perianth segments green, in 2 whorls of 4, lanceolate to linear. 8 stamens (rarely more). Fruit a black round berry to 1cm across, turning blue when ripe.
Flowering season: May-Jun
Habitat: Deciduous, rarely coniferous, woods
Distribution: Most of Europe; Asia. Widespread and local in Britain. Absent from Ireland.

2

Lords-and-Ladies*☠ *Arum maculatum*

(Arum Family)

Plant to 50cm tall. Leaves 10-20cm long, long-stalked and arrow-shaped with a network of veins. Inflorescence very distinctive. Purple-violet central spike (the spadix) surrounded by a 10-25cm long yellow-green, sometimes red-speckled bract (the spathe). A cluster of bright red berries develops from the flowers at the base of the spadix. Berries about 5mm in diameter.
Flowering season: Apr-May
Habitat: Deciduous and mixed woodland on damp, chalky humus-rich soils.
Distribution: Much of Europe, except the far N and E. In British Isles commonest in the S.
Note on Biology: Lords-and-Ladies has an unusual method of pollination. Small flies and midges are attracted to the flowers by their unpleasant smell (rather like rotting meat). Many of these slither down the slippery inner surface of the spathe and are then trapped in the lower flask-like chamber. The female flowers with ovary and stigmas surround the lower part of the spadix, the male flowers, each with 3-4 stamens, slightly higher up. There is also a ring of bristly hairs above and below the clusters of male flowers; these prevent the insects from leaving. As the insects fly about trying to escape they unwittingly pollinate the stigmas of the female flowers. The spathe gradually becomes less slippery and the bristly hairs shrivel up, thus allowing the pollen-laden insects to find their way out again.

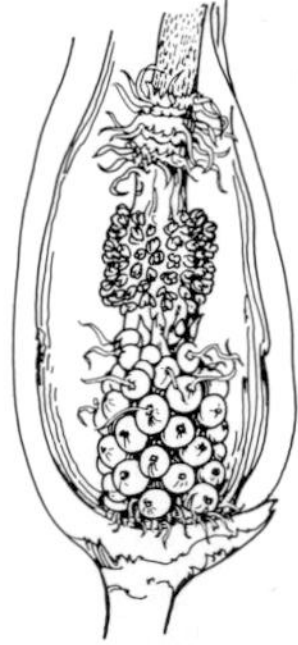

INFLORESCENCE
Lords-and-Ladies
(vertical section)

1
2

1

Sweet-flag*

Acorus calamus

(Arum Family)

Plant to 1.5m tall, with stiff, grass-like leaves, about 2cm wide. Stem triangular. Inflorescence a long spathe with a cylindrical greenish-yellow spadix pointing out to one side and up to about 9cm long. Spathe up to 10 times as long as the spadix. Flowers all very small and hermaphrodite. Perianth segments less than 1mm long and yellowish-green. Fruit a reddish berry.

Flowering season: May-Jul

Habitat: Still or slowflowing water with a muddy bottom. Reed beds and sedge communities

Distribution: Much of Europe; Asia; N America. Locally naturalized in lowland England.

2

Branched Bur-reed*

Sparganium erectum

(Bur-reed Family)

To 2m tall with triangular leaves up to 15mm wide. Stem branched. Male and female flowers in different, spherical inflorescences on the same plant, male inflorescences above female inflorescences. Flowers with scale-like perianth segments. Fruit 7-11mm long, beaked, with broad, flat upper part.

Flowering season: Jun-Aug

Habitat: Still or slowflowing water, ditches, marshes

Distribution: Most of Europe; Asia; N America.

Similar species: Floating Bur-reed*, *Sparganium angustifolium*, has leaves which are usually floating and stems to 1m long. Inflorescences unbranched. Mainly N Europe and mountainous areas, in pools and ditches. In British Isles mainly on high ground in N and W.

3

Common Reedmace*

Typha latifolia

(Reedmace Family)

Plant to 3m tall with broad flat leaves 10-20mm across. Male and female flowers very small and surrounded by long hairs at the base. These are clustered together in long cylindrical spikes in which the female flowers are towards the base.

Flowering season: Jul-Aug

Habitat: Still or slowflowing water with sandy bottom and up to 1.5m deep

Distribution: much of Europe; Asia; N America.

Similar species: Lesser Reedmace*, *T. angustifolia*, has leaves 3-10mm across and a noticeable gap on the stem between the male and female parts of the inflorescence.

1|2
3

1

Bee Orchid* ☒ *Ophrys apifera*

(Orchid Family)

Small orchid (to about 45cm). Flowers beautifully marked on lip and about 1.5cm long, resembling female bumble bee. Lip 3-lobed with 2 small, furry side-lobes. 2 inner perianth segments narrow and greenish.
Flowering season: Jun-Jul. *Habitat:* dry grassland, dunes; mainly on calcareous soils
Distribution: Mainly W Europe, from Holland southwards. Local in England, Wales and Ireland.
Similar species: Fly Orchid* ☒, *Ophrys insectifera.* 3 outer perianth segments oval, green 5-8mm long, 2 inner upper segments thread-like and brownish-red (like the antennae of an insect). Lip 10-15mm long, brown to reddish-brown and twice as long as wide; 3-lobed, middle lobe deeply indented at the tip.
Flowering season: May-Jun. *Habitat:* dry grassland, open pine woods.
Distribution: most of Europe. Rather scattered in N and W. Rare in Ireland, absent from Scotland and local and mainly southern in England and Wales.
Early Spider Orchid* ☒, *O. sphegodes.* Outer perianth segments oval 8-12mm long, yellowish green, 2 inner upper segments lanceolate, pale blue. Lip about as long as wide and only weakly 3-lobed; scarcely indented at tip. Dry grassland. C Europe north to S England. In Britain rare and only in S England, mainly coastal.

2

Bird's-nest Orchid* ☒ *Neottia nidus-avis*

(Orchid Family)

Hairless plant to 40cm tall with a simple stem and a rather strange yellowish-brown colour. 4-6 lanceolate leaves encircling stem. Inflorescence 5-15cm, many-flowered. Bracts narrowly lanceolate and half as long as ovaries. 5 upper perianth segments oval, 4-6mm long and brown. Lip 7-12mm long and divided into 2 lobes at the tip.
Flowering season: May-Jun
Habitat: Beech and mixed deciduous woods; mostly on calcareous soils
Distribution: Most of Europe; Siberia. In Britain commonest in S England.
Note on Biology: Bird's-nest Orchid is a saprophytic plant. It lives on organic substances of the woodland floor with the help of symbiotic fungi.

3

Common Twayblade* ☒ *Listera ovata*

(Orchid Family)

Hairless plant growing to 50cm tall, with unbranched stem and a pair of unstalked, rounded to broadly oval, basal leaves, each to 5-15cm long. Inflorescence many-flowered. Bracts oval, as long as ovaries. Upper 5 perianth segments rather blunt, 3-4mm and green. Lip yellowish-green, 6-8mm, narrowly wedge-shaped and deeply divided at the tip.
Flowering season: May-Jul
Habitat: Meadows, open deciduous and coniferous woods, mainly on calcareous soils
Distribution: Most of Europe; N Asia.
Similar species: Lesser Twayblade* ☒, *Listera cordata* . Plant to 20cm tall, leaves triangular or heart-shaped, to 3cm long. Inflorescence few-flowered. Outer perianth segments green, lip red, to 4mm long. Coniferous woods. In British Isles mainly in N and W.

1

2|3

1

Asarabacca* ☠ ☒

Asarum europaeum

(Birthwort Family)

Plant to 10cm tall with a creeping stem covered with soft, pale hairs. Leaves dark green and kidney-shaped with a leathery surface. Flowers solitary and terminal. Corolla bell-shaped, 3-lobed, fused at the base and 1-1.5cm long, greenish on the outside and reddish-brown inside.
Flowering season: Apr-May
Habitat: Mixed deciduous woods, mostly on calcareous soils
Distribution: Most of Europe; N Asia. In Britain rather rare and decreasing.

2

Stinging Nettle*

Urtica dioica

(Nettle Family)

Dioecious plant to 1.5m tall, covered with stinging hairs. Leaves opposite, heartshaped at the base and broadly toothed. Inflorescence clustered in the leaf axils. 4 inconspicuous small greenish bracts.
Flowering season: Jul-Oct. *Habitat:* Footpaths, waste ground, clearings
Distribution: Worldwide.
Similar species: Annual Nettle°, *U. urens,* has rounded leaves, wedge-shaped at the base.

3

Hop* ✿

Humulus lupulus

(Hemp Family)

A roughly-hairy climbing plant growing to about 6m. Leaves stalked, opposite, mostly 3-7 lobed and heart-shaped at the base. Male flowers in a many flowered panicle. Female flowers cone-like, with oval bracts up to 2cm long. Pale green.
Flowering season: Jul-Sep. *Habitat:* Wet woodlands and scrub
Distribution: Most of Europe; N Asia; N America. Widely cultivated for flavouring beer.

4

Sheep's Sorrel*

Rumex acetosella

(Dock Family)

Plant to 40cm tall with linear, stalked leaves, arrow-shaped at base with 2 pointed basal lobes. Inflorescence an open panicle. Flowers with bracts. Perianth segments small, greenish and 6-lobed. Flower dioecious. Male flowers with 6 stamens, female flowers with 3 stigmas on the ovary.
Flowering season: May-Jul
Habitat: Fields on acid soils, grassland, heaths, dunes, footpaths
Distribution: Most of Europe; W Asia.

5

Curled Dock*

Rumex crispus

(Dock Family)

Hairless plant to 1m tall. Leaves broadly lanceolate, with curled edges. Lower leaves long-stalked. Outer 3 perianth segments small, inner 3, 3.5-4.5mm long and enclosing the triangular nut in fruit. Fruit valves untoothed.
Flowering season: May-Jul. *Habitat:* Weed communities
Distribution: Worldwide. Very common In British Isles.
Similar species: Broad-leaved Dock°, *R. obtusifolius,* has broader lower leaves, and fruit valves with long teeth. Very common in British Isles.

1|2
3
4|5

1

Black Bindweed* *Polygonum convolvulus*

(Dock Family)

Climbing, twisting plant to 1m, with stalked arrowshaped leaves to 8cm long. Flowers in few-flowered spikes. 5 pale green perianth segments, the outer 3 keeled along back. Fruit a black, triangular nut, enclosed by bracts.
Flowering season: Jul-Sep
Habitat: Fields, gardens, crops, waste ground
Distribution: Worldwide.

2

Good King Henry* *Chenopodium bonus-henricus*

(Goosefoot Family)

Mainly unbranched, sparsely hairy plant growing to 80cm tall. Leaves stalked and spear-shaped, up to 10cm long. Inflorescence a dense terminal spike. 3-5 small green perianth segments with toothed margins. 5 stamens. Fruit with fleshy wall and one shiny seed.
Flowering season: May-Oct
Habitat: Footpaths, weed communities, pastures, waste ground
Distribution: Most of Europe. Introduced and locally common in British Isles; originally used as a vegetable.

3

Glasswort* *Salicornia europaea*

(Goosefoot Family)

Branched, hairless plant to about 30cm tall, with segmented stem, surrounded by the fleshy sheath-like unstalked leaves. Inflorescence a fleshy spike. Flowers tiny, in 3's in the axils of the upper leaves.
Flowering season: Aug-Oct
Habitat: Saltmarshes and mud flats; inland salt areas
Distribution: N Hemisphere. Locally common around coasts of British Isles.

4

Prickly Saltwort* *Salsola kali*

(Goosefoot Family)

Somewhat branched plant to about 1m tall. Leaves narrowly triangular, with a yellow spine. 5 erect perianth segments with a veined, fleshy wing along the back. Flowers solitary in the leaf axils.
Flowering season: Jul-Sep. *Habitat:* Sea coasts, salty sand
Distribution: Europe east to C Asia. Frequent around sandy coasts of British Isles.

5

Common Orache* *Atriplex patula*

(Goosefoot Family)

Plant to about 1m tall, often with a mealy covering. Leaves mainly alternate, lanceolate and stalked. Inflorescence in long spikes. Male flowers small with 3-5 petals. Female flowers lacking perianth segments and with 2 bracts fused at the base.
Flowering season: Jul-Oct. *Habitat:* fields, paths, waste ground
Distribution: Most of Europe, Asia, N America. Common throughout British Isles.
Similar species: Spear-leaved Orache*, *A. prostrata,* has mainly opposite leaves, lower ones triangular and spear-shaped. Bracts of female flowers with several teeth at edges.

1|2
3
4|5

1

Pigweed

Amaranthus lividus

(Amaranth Family)

Low-growing, hairless annual plant to 45cm, with alternate, rhombic leaves to 5cm long. Inflorescenses in leaf axils or in terminal panicle. Flowers with 3 perianth segments. Fruit not opening.
Flowering season: Jun-Oct
Habitat: Farmland, footpaths, waste ground
Distribution: Virtually worldwide, in warmer regions, but vary rarely recorded in Britain.

2

Smooth Rupturewort* ☒

Herniaria glabra

(Pink Family)

Prostrate, creeping plant with much-branched stem. Leaves 3-8mm long, opposite and oval, with fleshy stipules. Flowers small, rounded, and unstalked, in the leaf axils. 5 greete border. Petals absent.
Flowering season: May-Sep. *Habitat:* Acid sandy soils, fields, footpaths
Distribution: Most of Europe. In BI, mainly in E England; rare elsewhere.

3

Annual Knawel*

Scleranthus annuus

(Pink Family)

Small annual or biennial plant to 20cm tall, branched towards top. Leaves opposite, linear, to 1.5cm long. Flowers tiny and clustered at tips of stems. Sepals 5, 3 4.5mm long, narrowly lanceolate, with very narrow, white border. Petals absent.
Flowering season: May-Sep. *Habitat:* acid sandy soils, fields, footpaths
Distribution: most of Europe. Widespread in Britain; rare in Ireland.

4

Lady's-Mantle*

Alchemilla

(Rose Family)

This is a genus of pretty plants with characteristically palmately lobed or divided, toothed leaves, and clusters of tiny, yellowish green flowers. The flowers have green sepals and lack petals. There are many species in the region and they can only be reliably identified by the expert, using detailed floras.
The species shown, *Alchemilla monticola*°, is a hairy plant, growing to about 30cm. The leaves are rounded, 3-10cm across, with 7-9 toothed lobes.
Flowering season: May-Sep. *Habitat:* Poor meadows and pastures
Distribution: Europe, E to Siberia. Common in much of C Europe, but quite rare in England (Weardale and Teesdale).

5

Stinking Hellebore* ☠ ❀

Helleborus foetidus

(Buttercup Family)

Hairless plant to 50cm tall, with a thick, branched stem. Leaves 3- to 9-lobed, lower leaves stalked and up to 30cm across, the upper leaves smaller. Leaf lobes lanceolate and toothed. Flowers in a panicle. Flower about 1-2cm across, drooping and globular, with 5 rounded, green petal-like sepals. Fruits 3-5 many-seeded follicles, to 2cm long.
Flowering season: Mar-Apr. *Habitat:* Dry slopes, scrub, open woods
Distribution: S, W and C Europe. In Britain native mainly in S England and Wales, but commonly grown in gardens.

1|2
3|4
5

1

Round-leaved Sundew* *Drosera rotundifolia*

(Sundew Family)

To about 30cm tall (usually smaller), with unstalked stems, and a rosette of long-stalked, spoon-shaped leaves. Leaf blade 5-10mm broad, with sticky glandular hairs above and along edges. Hairs 1-5mm long. Stem leafless, with a few-flowered inflorescence. Sepals 5, short and fused at base. Petals 4-6mm long, white; flowers often not opening fully, and self-pollinating in the bud. Fruit a smooth capsule.

Flowering season: Jun-Aug. *Habitat:* Bogs, moors, wet heaths

Distribution: Europe, Siberia, N America. In Britain commonest in N and W.

Similar species: Great Sundew°, *D. anglica*, has longer, erect, narrower leaves (blade 5-10 times as long as broad) and smooth capsule. In British Isles commonest in NW Ireland and NW Scotland.

Oblong-leaved Sundew°, *D. intermedia*, has erect, spoon-shaped leaves (blades 2-3 times as long as broad). Capsule with longitudinal furrows. In British Isles mainly in W Scotland and W Ireland.

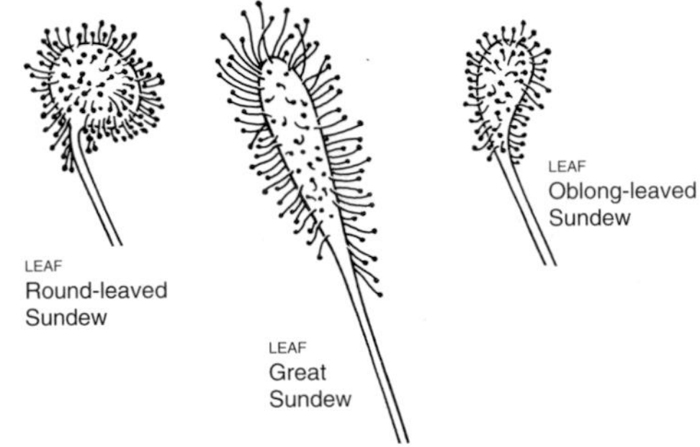

2

Dog's Mercury* ☠ *Mercurialis perennis*

(Spurge Family)

Single-stemmed plant to 40cm tall. Leaves opposite, coarsely toothed and lanceolate, about 4-12cm long and crowded together towards top of stem. Dioecious. Male plants have a many-flowered spike of small, green flowers, each with 3-lobed calyx and 8 to 20 stamens (no petals). Female plants with clusters of flowers in leaf axils, each with a 2-celled ovary, each with a single seed. Fruit stalk several times longer than fruit.

Flowering season: Apr-May

Habitat: Shady deciduous woods, mainly on calcareous soils

Distribution: Europe, SW Asia.

Similar species: Annual Mercury°, *M. annua*, is a smaller, annual plant with branched stems and leaves evenly distributed. Fruit stalk shorter than fruit. Rich weedy habitats, including gardens, fields.

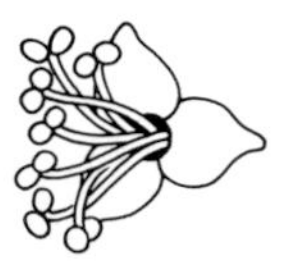

1

2

1

Sun Spurge* ☠ *Euphorbia helioscopia*

(Spurge Family)

Usually branched annual, growing to 40cm tall, with milky juice. Leaves opposite, ovate to spoon-shaped and finely toothed at the tip. Inflorescence umbel-like, with 3 to 5 main branches or rays. Flower heads resemble single flowers, being cup-shaped with 4 oval, yellow glands around margin, each surrounded by 2 unfused bracts. Fruit a 2.5-3mm round capsule, opening into 3 valves.

Flowering season: Apr-Jun

Habitat: Weedy habitats, gardens, fields

Distribution: Europe, Asia.

2

Wood Spurge* ☠ ❀ *Euphorbia amygdaloides*

(Spurge Family)

Perennial to 70cm tall, producing sterile as well as flowering stems. Milky juice. Leaves leathery and lanceolate, entire. Inflorescence umbel-like with 5-9 rays. Upper bracts rounded and fused. Flower head structure similar to previous species.

Flowering season: Apr-Jun

Habitat: Deciduous woods, on calcareous soils

Distribution: Europe, except N and E; W Asia. In Britain mainly in S England and Wales.

3

Mare's-tail* *Hippuris vulgaris*

(Mare's-tail Family)

Water plant with stems to 2m long and mostly upright flowering stems, growing up above the water. Leaves linear and entire, in whorls of 4 to 20. Flowers small and in leaf axils, consisting of just a single stamen or ovary (male and female flowers may be separate or flowers hermaphrodite).

Flowering season: May-Aug

Habitat: Still or slow-flowing water

Distribution: Virtually worldwide.

4

Sea Holly* *Eryngium maritimum*

(Carrot Family)

Branched, thorny and hairless plant to 50cm tall, with waxy, 3- to 5-lobed spiny leaves. Upper leaves enveloping stem. Flowers many, in dense rounded umbels. Bracts oval, 3-lobed and spiny.

Flowering season: Jun-Aug

Habitat: Coastal sand and shingle

Distribution: Coasts of Europe, N to S Norway. N Africa; common round coasts of British Isles, except N and E Scotland.

Similar species: Field Eryngo* ⊠, *Eryngium campestre*, is a species of dry grassland. It has 3-lobed, twice pinnate spiny leaves and linear-lanceolate spiny bracts below flower heads. C and S Europe. Rare plant in S England.

1|2
3
4

1

Common Figwort* *Scrophularia nodosa*

(Figwort Family)

Erect plant to 80cm tall, with rectangular, unwinged stems. Leaves paired, short-stalked, oval, pointed and coarsely toothed. Flowers in much-branched inflorescence. Individual flowers are greenish-brown, about 10mm long, with a purple upper lip, 4 stamens and a 5-lobed calyx.
Flowering season: Jun-Sep
Habitat: Damp woods, hedges
Distribution: Throughout Europe, except far N. Rare or absent from far N of Scotland.
Similar species: Water Figwort*, *S. auriculata*, has a 4-winged stem, and pale-bordered calyx lobes. Mainly W Europe. In British Isles rarer towards N and W.
Green Figwort* ☒, *S. umbrosa*, has broadly winged stems and sharply toothed leaves. Damp places from Scotland and Denmark, southwards. Rare and local in Ireland and Britain.

2

Common Broomrape* *Orobanche minor*

(Broomrape Family)

Strange-looking plant lacking chlorophyll and growing to about 50cm tall. Broomrapes are parasitic on the roots of their hosts, this species usually on roots of legumes, particularly clovers. Stem is an erect spike of reddish-purple or yellowish flowers, spaced increasingly widely towards the base. Upper lip of flower notched, lower lip with 3 lobes.
Flowering season: Jun-Sep
Habitat: Grassland
Distribution: Mainly C and S Europe. S and E Ireland and lowland England.
Similar species: Knapweed Broomrape*, *O. elatior*, is larger, with bigger, more densely clustered flowers. Its host is Greater Knapweed, *Centaurea scabiosa* (see p 154). Scattered from S Sweden southwards. In Britain mainly in S and E England and S Wales.

3

Toothwort* *Lathraea squamaria*

(Figwort Family)

Another odd-looking parasitic plant lacking chlorophyll. To about 20cm, with unbranched stem and pinkish, scale-like leaves. Flowers densely clustered in a slightly drooping one-sided spike. Calyx 9-12mm long and 4-lobed, hairy. Corolla a pale violet short tube with 2-lobed upper lip and 3-lobed lower lip. Parasitic on trees and shrubs such as Hazel.
Flowering season: Apr-May
Habitat: Damp deciduous woods
Distribution: Europe, Asia. Absent from much of Ireland (except E) and N Scotland.
Note on Biology: Toothwort is a parasite of trees and shrubs. It takes in all the water, minerals and organic nutrients it needs from the roots of its host.

1|2

3

1

Crosswort* *Cruciata laevipes*

(Bedstraw Family)

Hairy plant to 50cm tall, with rather delicate stems. Leaves narrowly lanceolate, 3-veined and in cross-shaped whorls of 4. Flowers in clusters of 3 to 7, in axils of upper leaves. Bracts small. Calyx absent. Corolla 4-lobed, 1.5-2.5mm across, pale yellow. Fruits 1.5-2.5mm across, wrinkled, black when ripe.
Flowering season: Apr-Jun
Habitat: Meadows, woodland margins, footpaths
Distribution: Europe, N to Holland, N Germany and Britain. Asia.

2

Hoary Plantain* *Plantago media*

(Plantain Family)

To 30cm tall, with a rosette of basal leaves. Leaves elliptic, weakly toothed, short-stemmed and with short hairs on either side. Stem curving upwards with terminal dense, cylindrical spike of scented flowers. 4 sepals, fused at base. Corolla 4mm long, tube-shaped, with 4 pointed lobes. Fruit a 3- to 8-seeded capsule, opening at top.
Flowering season: May-Sep
Habitat: Dry grassland, especially calcareous
Distribution: Europe, N Asia. In Britain commonest in S and C England.

3

Greater Plantain* *Plantago major*

(Plantain Family)

Weakly hairy plant to 40cm tall. Leaves in basal rosette. Leaves long, broadly oval, rounded or heart-shaped at base and 5-9 veined. Spike dense, cylindrical and up to 10cm long, reaching even 20cm in fruit. 4 sepals, unfused. Corolla yellowish, tube-shaped, with 4 lobes. Fruit a capsule, opening at top, usually with 8 seeds.
Flowering season: Jun-Oct
Habitat: Footpaths, damp meadows, pastures, lawns
Distribution: Spread worldwide.
Note on Biology: Greater Plantain is a classic ruderal plant, colonising waste ground and footpaths, and extremely tolerant of trampling. The small seeds have an absorbent outer layer. When damp, they become sticky and cling to the feet of animals and people, and thus get dispersed. In N America this species followed soon after the Europeans appeared and came to be known to the native Americans as "White Man's Footsteps".

4

Ribwort Plantain* *Plantago lanceolata*

(Plantain Family)

Hairless or slightly hairy plant to 30cm all. Leaves lanceolate, in basal rosette, erect, with obvious longitudinal veins. Flowers small, heads rounded at first, becoming cylindrical, on long stalks. Calyx and corolla 4-lobed. Fruit a 2-seeded capsule, opening at top.
Flowering season: Apr-Sep
Habitat: Meadows, pastures, footpaths, lawns
Distribution: Europe. Spread worldwide.

1|2
3
4

1

Moschatel, Townhall Clock*

(Moschatel Family) *Adoxa moschatellina*

Small, delicate, musk-scented plant with unbranched stem to 15cm tall. Leaves twice 3-lobed. Basal leaves long-stalked, the 2 stem leaves short-stalked. Heads with 5 flowers, each greenish and about 5mm across. Terminal flower with 4-lobed corolla, side flowers with 5-lobed corollas. Stamens equal in number to corolla lobes, but each divided into 2, giving the impression of 8 or 10 per flower.
Flowering season: Mar-May. *Habitat:* Woods, scrub
Distribution: Europe; Asia; N America. Absent from Ireland.

2

Small Teasel* ☒ *Dipsacus pilosus*

(Teasel Family)

Bristly, branched plant growing to 1.5m. Leaves oval and toothed, long-stalked at base, short-stalked on stem. Flower heads dense, spherical and 2-2.5cm in diameter. Bracts lanceolate and bristly. Epicalyx and calyx toothed, the latter bowl-shaped. Corolla 4-lobed with a tube of 5-7mm.
Flowering season: Jul-Aug. *Habitat:* Footpaths, waste ground, wood margins
Distribution: Europe, W Asia. Absent from Ireland and Scotland and rather rare in England and Wales.

3

Pineappleweed* *Matricaria matricarioides*

(Daisy Family)

Aromatic plant, smelling of pineapple when crushed. To 40cm, hairless, branched. Leaves 2 to 3 times divided. Flower heads 5-10mm across with bare involucral bracts. Ray florets absent. Tube florets 4-lobed at tip, greenish.
Flowering season: Jun-Aug. *Habitat:* Footpaths, waste ground
Distribution: Spread worldwide. Introduced into Britain from N America in late 19th century, and now throughout British Isles.

4

Common Cudweed* *Filago vulgaris*

(Daisy Family)

Softly hairy plant to 35cm tall, with upright stem, branched in upper third. Leaves narrowly lanceolate, to 2.5cm long, with wavy margins. Flower heads small, rounded clusters of 20 to 40 flowers. Ray florets absent. About 25 thread-shaped female florets and 2-3 hermaphrodite tube florets per flower head.
Flowering season: Jul-Sep. *Habitat:* Dry grassy places, footpaths, sandy ground
Distribution: W, C and S Europe.

5

Highland Cudweed* ☒ *Gnaphalium norvegicum*

(Daisy Family)

Unbranched plant to 40cm tall, covered with felty hairs. Leaves narrow, lanceolate and 3-veined. Flower heads small, clustered in leaf axils in loose spike. Bracts long, with dark brown margins.
Flowering season: Jul-Sep *Habitat:* Open woods, grassy slopes
Distribution: N and C Europe, Alps and other mountains; Siberia. In Britain a rare plant of Scottish mountains.
Similar species: Marsh Cudweed*, *G. uliginosum*, bushy with dense, woolly hairs and clustered dark brown flower heads. Damp, disturbed ground.

1|2
3
4|5

1

Mugwort*

Artemisia vulgaris

(Daisy Family)

Branched plant, to about 1.3m tall, with an unpleasant smell. Stem angled, branched and weakly hairy. Leaves green and hairless above, covered with grey or white felty hairs below, and 1 to 2 times divided, with lanceolate, toothed lobes. Lower leaves stalked, upper leaves stalkless. Flower heads very small, ovoid, 3-4mm long and arranged in a many-headed panicle. Few flowers in each head, either yellowish or reddish-brown. Inner florets tube-form and hermaphrodite, outer florets thread-like and female.

Flowering season: Jul-Sep

Habitat: Footpaths, waste ground, river banks

Distribution: Spread almost worldwide.

Similar species: Wormwood°, *A. absinthium*, is strongly aromatic and bitter-tasting, with silky hairs and drooping, slightly larger flower heads. Europe, Asia. Introduced widely as medicinal plant, or for flavourings. Sea Wormwood°, *A. maritimum*, is smaller (to about 60cm), with small, twice pinnate leaves, flower heads only about 2-3mm long and lacking thread-shaped female florets. Mainly coastal in W Europe, and in salty sites inland.

2

Butterbur*

Petasites hybridus

(Daisy Family)

Erect dioecious plant with flower spikes to 40cm tall, reaching up to 1m tall when in fruit. Plant with grey, felty hairs. Leaves stalked, very large and up to 60cm across, heart-shaped and toothed. Stem leaves scale-like. Flower heads in cylindrical spikes. Florets tubular, with reddish corolla. Female florets about 5mm across, male about 1cm across. Fruit with white, hairy pappus, to 1cm long.

Flowering season: Mar-May

Habitat: River and stream sides, wet alder scrub, damp waste ground

Distribution: Most of Europe, except far N; N and W Asia. In the British Isles, male plants are locally common, while female plants occur mainly in N England.

Similar species: White Butterbur°, *P. albus*, has smaller leaves and yellowish flowers. In Britain introduced and local.

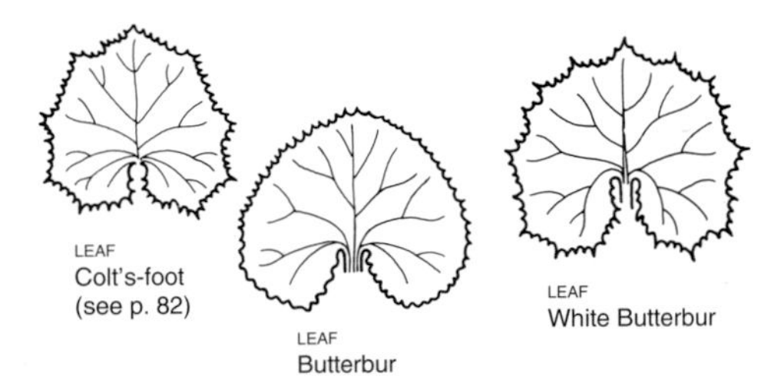

1
2

1

Cabbage Thistle

Cirsium oleraceum

(Daisy Family)

Branched plant to 1.5m tall, with soft, weakly spiny leaves. Leaves oval, undivided or deeply divided, with lanceolate, toothed lobes and hairless or weakly hairy. Lower leaves stalked, upper leaves with heart-shaped bases clasping stem. Flower heads terminal and surrounded by pale green bracts. Involucre 1.5-2cm long, brownish. Florets all tubular, with 1.5-2cm long pale yellow corollas. Fruits 4mm long, pale grey, with feathery pappus.

Flowering season: Jun-Aug

Habitat: Damp meadows, fens, wet woods, river banks

Distribution: Most of Europe except N and W. In Britain only as an occasional introduction.

2

Carline Thistle*

Carlina vulgaris

(Daisy Family)

Hairy plant to 30cm tall, with branched stem. Basal leaves 6-8cm long, lanceolate and with spiny lobes. Upper leaves stalkless, grey-green above and softly hairy below, with spiny teeth. Flower heads stalked, solitary or in small groups of 2 or 3, each 3-5cm across. Florets surrounded by long, yellowish involucral bracts, spreading out like a star. Florets numerous, all tube-type and yellowish. Fruits with 7-8mm long pappus, consisting of 10-12 feathery bristles.

Flowering season: Jul-Aug

Habitat: Dry grassland, open woods

Distribution: Europe, except far N. In British Isles, very characteristic of calcareous grassland.

1
2

Botany in Brief

The flowering plants are the largest group in the plant kingdom, with more than 250,000 species so far described. The most important features of flowering plants are the following:
division of the plant into root, stem and leaves; possession of flowers; development of seeds. For this reason the flowering plants are also often known as seed plants. The extraordinary diversity of flower-shape originates mainly from adaptations to pollination – wind pollination, and particularly insect pollination. Through their 100 million year history, most flowering plants have evolved in close association with insects, and this is certainly one reason why these two groups are amongst the most species-rich in the plant and animal kingdoms. Although flowering plants exist in a bewildering variety of forms, they are all built according to a similar plan, consisting of the three basic organs – root, shoot and leaf.

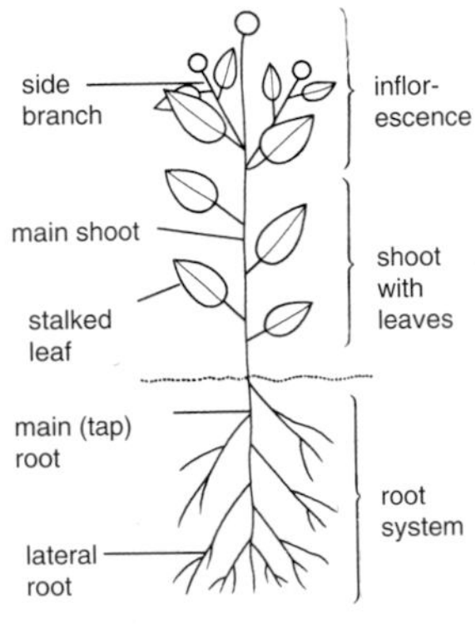

SCHEMATIC DIAGRAM OF A PLANT

THE ROOT

Roots serve to anchor a plant in the soil and to facilitate the uptake of water and mineral salts. They normally grow deep in the soil and are leafless. They are thus distinguished from pale underground stems, which carry leaf-scales.
The *main or tap root* is normally vertical in the soil. From this grow *lateral roots*, which may themselves branch. In this way the full root system develops.

THE SHOOT

The shoot or stem is made up of *internodes*, separated by *nodes*. The leaves arise at these nodes, which are often somewhat thickened. Sometimes the stem remains unbranched, but there are usually *side branches* as well, emerging from buds in the leaf axils. The side branches may themselves branch, resulting in a *shoot system*.
Shoots continue to grow at the tip, and develop new leaves, with buds in the axils, which can grow into branches. Like the leaves, the stem can either be hairless, or it may carry hairs of various kinds.
The following types of hair can be distinguished, according to their texture:
bristles: simple, stiff, often pricking
felted: matted together, soft

downy: scattered, delicate
rough: strong, long, patent
silky: appressed, soft, shiny
woolly: soft, curved, often long
ciliate: many-celled hairs
glandular hairs: stalked glands

Structure of the shoot

There are many different kinds of shoot. *Stolons* grow horizontally above or below the ground and develop small roots. New plants may grow at their tips, in which case they are sometimes called *runners*. Some parts of the shoot may develop *tendrils*, which help support climbing plants. *Bulbs* are undergound stems with compressed, fleshy leaves storing water and nutrients. *Stem-tubers* are the swollen tips of stolons, again with a storage function. *Round* stems have a circular cross-section. Stems may also be *angled*, *furrowed* or *winged* when the angles carry thin extensions.

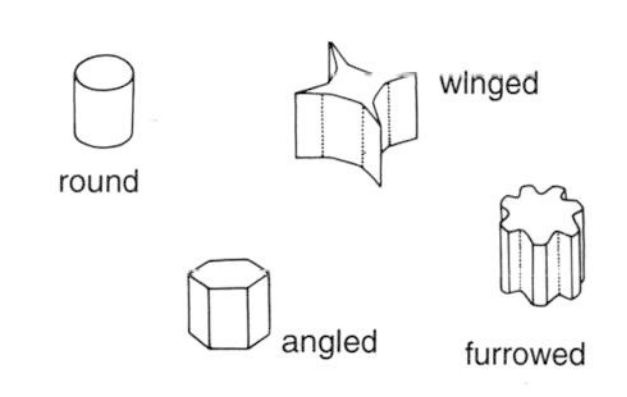

STEM CROSS SECTIONS

Longevity

Botanists distinguish between annuals, biennials and perennials. *Annuals* complete their life-cycle (germination, growth, flowering and seed production) within a year. *Biennials* grow without flowering in the first year, coming into flower in the second year. Both these groups are herbs which flower only once, produce seeds, and then die. *Perennials* by contrast flower for several or many years in succession. Some perennials have herbaceous above-ground foliage, and die back after producing seeds. Others die back to a woody stem-base, sending out fresh shoots the following spring. In *woody plants* (trees and shrubs) the whole shoot system is woody and permanent.

THE LEAF

Leaves are normally flat structures, coloured green by the chlorophyll they contain. Using this pigment, they are able to manufacture their own vital sugars and starch from carbon dioxide in the air and water.

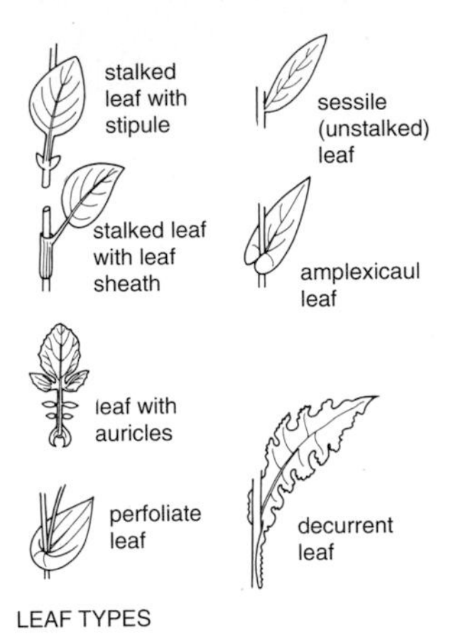

LEAF TYPES

Leaf position

Leaves grow as lateral appendages of the stem, from nodes. When there is a single leaf at each node, and successive leaves are not directly above each other, we speak of *alternate* leaves. If there are two leaves, one at each side of the node, they are termed *opposite*, although the pairs of leaves at successive nodes may be set at right angles to each other. When there are three or more leaves at each node, they are described as *whorled*, or in whorls.

Leaf structure

A fully developed leaf consists of the *blade*, the *leafstalk* (petiole), and *leaf base*. Sometimes there is no leafstalk, in which case the leaf is termed *sessile*, or unstalked; otherwise it is known as *petiolate*, or stalked. The leaf base is often inconspicuous, but sometimes has a *leaf sheath*, or *stipules* associated with it. Unstalked leaves may narrow towards the stem. Those partially encircling the stem with the leaf bases are called *sheathing* leaves. In other cases, the leaf base may have blunt or pointed extensions at either side of the stem (*amplexicaul*), or even completely encircle the stem (*perfoliate*). In *decurrent* leaves, the leaf blade extends some distance down the sides of the stem.

Leaf shapes

Leaves can be many different *shapes*, and these shapes are often important taxonomic characters. There are *simple* leaves with undivided blade, and *compound* leaves. Some have *parallel* or curved veins, without a central midrib; others have *pinnate* veins, with an obvious midrib and lateral veins. A leaf can have any one of a number of shapes, including: *linear*, *lanceolate*, *elliptic*, *ovate*, *hastate* (spear-shaped), *reniform* (kidney-shaped), *cordate* (heart-shaped), *rhombic*, *spatulate* or *spathulate*

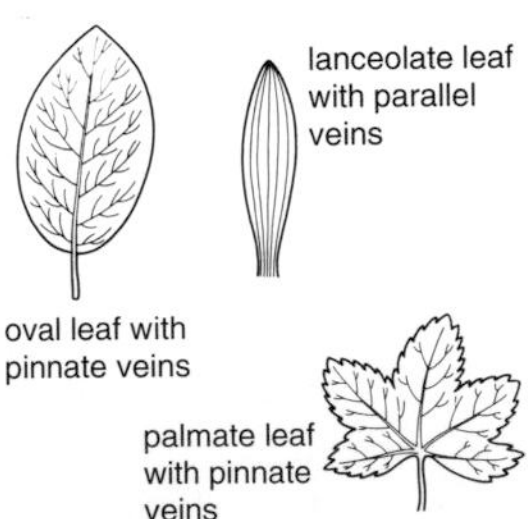

LEAF SHAPES AND VEINS

(spoon-shaped) or *sagittate* (arrow-shaped) (see page 256). There are also differences in leaf *margins*, including: *entire*, *crenate* (bluntly toothed margins), *serrate* (serated), *dentate* (toothed), *sinuate/undulate* (wavy margins), *pinnately lobed*, or *palmately lobed*.

a truncate
b rounded
c emarginate
d obtuse
e pointed
f mucronate

LEAF TIPS

There is just as much variation in the *shapes of compound leaves*. Their leaves consist of several separate leaflets. When these leaflets are paired along the central stem, the leaves are known as *pinnate* (*imparipinnate* if there is a terminal leaflet and *paripinnate* if not).

Specially adapted leaves

As with the root and stem, leaves have been specially adapted in a number of ways. *Thorns* are leaves in which the leaf blade does not develop, but in which the central nerve or midrib is thickened and pointed. *Scale leaves* are small, often pale leaves on underground stems. *Bracts* are leaves associated with an inflorescence. *Tendrils* are very narrow leaves, adapted for twining or clasping.

THE INFLORESCENCE

That part of the stem which carries the flower is known as the inflorescence. In rare cases, a shoot has just a single flower at its tip, but more often there are several or many flowers, arranged in a number of different ways (see inside back cover).

A *spike* is a flowerhead in which the individual flowers are stalkless. It can be short and dense, or long and loose. A *raceme* consists of stalked flowers, the stalks being unbranched and arising from the axils of bracts on the main flowering stem. Some racemes are, however, bractless (e.g. in the Cabbage family). A *panicle* is an inflorescence whose main branches are themselves branched. In an *umbel*, the flower stalks are of equal length and arise from the same point on the stem. Umbels are often *compound*, with several partial umbels on stalks of equal length.

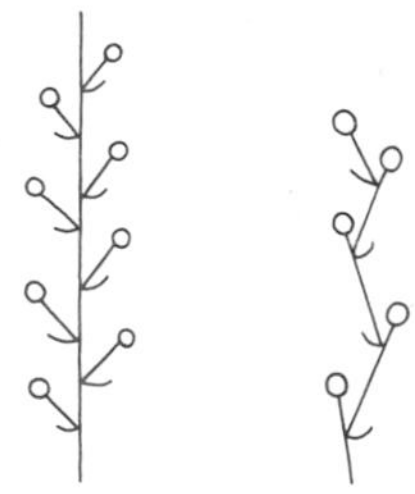

INFLORESCENCES

A *head* consists of many unstalked or short-stalked flowers growing close together at the end of a stem. The particularly densely-clustered head of composites is known as a *capitulum*. In it the individual flowers grow from the expanded end of a stem and are surrounded by an involucre.

All these types of inflorescence have a central main stem and are known as *racemose*. Inflorescences with branched stems, each ending in a single flower, are called *cymose*.

THE FLOWER

Flower structure

The flower (see p. 1) is a thickened shoot which carries the reproductive parts of the plant. Its individual parts are modified leaves. The *perianth* consists either of *perianth segments*, or of *sepals* and *petals*. The male part of the flower (*androecium*) consists of the *stamens*; the female part (*gynoecium*) consists of the *ovary*, *style* and *stigma*, together know as the *pistil*.

The perianth

The parts of a flower usually have a circular arrangement, and may sometimes overlap each other.
This may best be appreciated with reference to a basic floral diagram. The *perianth segments* make up the outer (lower) ring. More commonly, these are differentiated into an outer ring of usually green sepals (the *calyx*), and an inner ring of usually coloured petals (the *corolla*). The *sepals* may be either free or fused together. The fused part is called the *calyx tube* or *calyx cup*, with free *calyx teeth* or *calyx lobes*. Sometimes the calyx is surrounded by an *epicalyx* of bracts.
The *petals*, collectively called the *corolla*, form the next ring. Their colour serves to attract pollinating insects, as do the scent and the sugary nectar secreted by the *nectaries*.
Sometimes there is a *spur* at the base of the petals, which may act as a reservoir for nectar. The petals may also be free, or fused together. Some flowers, particularly those pollinated by wind, have reduced petals or may even lack petals altogether.

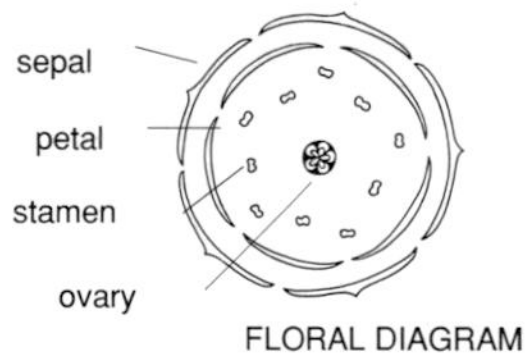

FLORAL DIAGRAM

Reproductive parts

Next in from the perianth is a ring or rings of *stamens*. Each stamen consists of a thin *filament* and an *anther*, the latter containing the *pollen*. In the centre of the flower is the *pistil* (gynoecium). This consists of at least one *carpel*, often more, either free or fused. The pistil is divided into *ovary*, *style* and *stigma*. The ovary may be *superior* (that is above the perianth base) or *inferior* (below the perianth base). It may also be *intermediate* in position.

Symmetry

If a flower has more than 1 axis of symmetry it is known as radially symmetrical. Flowers with a single axis of symmetry are bilaterally symmetrical, and the perianth is often divided into an *upper*- and a *lower-lip*. Flowers which are only male or female (contain either only stamens or only carpels) are called *unisexual*.

THE FRUIT

The fruit develops from the *ovary*, after pollination. It protects the seeds until they are ripe and often also has particular adaptations for seed dispersal. Its morphology is dependent, among other things, on the number of carpels and their arrangement. There are many different kinds of fruit (see inside front cover).

Dehiscent fruits

These are fruits which open to release the seeds. A *follicle* develops from a single carpel and splits open along one side only. A *legume* opens along both sides. A *capsule* is formed from more than one carpel. There are many types of capsule, including those with pores, teeth, or which open along clefts, or which split around the middle. One type of capsule is the *siliqua*, which consists of two carpels whose fused edges carry the seeds, and a central, papery partition. The siliqua opens when the two outer edges bend upwards away from the partition. Siliquas less than three times as long as broad are called *siliculas*.

Indehiscent fruits

These are fruits which do not open, and which are therefore dispersed with their seeds. A *nut* is usually single-seeded and has a hard covering. A small, indehiscent, single-seeded nut may be called an *achene*. Fleshy fruits with a central, hard, 'stone' seed are called *drupes*. In a *berry*, the whole fruit wall is fleshy. Some fruits split into many parts when ripe. *Multiple*, or *compound* fruits develop from many, separate carpels. Indehiscent fruits may have special modifications for dispersal. Examples are *winged fruits*, and those with feathery outgrowths (e.g. the pappus which develops from the modified calyx in composites).

INDEX

THE PHOTOGRAPHS

Bellmann: 21/1, 51/1, 57/1, 113/2, 157/4, 169/1, 179/2, 183/3, 197/2, 199/2, 203/2; Bolze: 167/1; Bormann: 95/1, UI (1); Buff: 57/3; Cuveland: 191/4, 203/3; Dähncke: 53/3; Danesch: 33/2, 39/4, 97/4, 99/3, 125/1, 145/1, 217/2, 233/5; Daudt: 137/2, 219/1, 233/1; Diedrich: 117/1, 123/1, 129/4, 131/2, 137/4, 193/1; Eichinger: 145/4, 201/1; Eigstler: 11/1, 65/1, U4 (1); Eisenbeiß: 23/1, 61/2, 75/1, 99/1,2, 123/2, U1 (1); Andrew N. Gagg, Photo Flora: 19/4, 33/1, 63/2, 3, 81/2, 91/4, 5, 97/2, 149/4; Garnweidner: 9/3, 13/3, 15/3; Glader: 63/5; Photocenter Greiner & Meyer: 97/3, 111/2, 171/2, 183/1; Harms: 37/2, 67/1, 105/2, 199/1, 3, 215/2, 231/2; Helo: 19/2, 205/3, 221/1; Hinz: 55/1, 107/2, 135/1; E & D Hosking: 25/1, 85/1, 85/4, 155/2; G E Hyde: 169/4; R. König 23/2, 43/3, 49/1, 129/3, 171/1, 177/1, 227/4; Kohlhaupt: 17/2, 37/1, 53/2, 179/1, 197/1; Krebs: 85/3, 95/4, 109/3, 121/1, 4, 157/2; Lauber: 23/4, 45/1, 65/4, 91/2, 101/1, 145/3, 207/2, 219/4, 221/2, 229/1; W. Lippert: 191/3; Marktanner: 29/3, 31/4, 45/5, 69/3, 77/1, 192/2; Baud Con Maydell: 181/2; Moosrainer: 143/1; Munker: 121/2, 149/1, 153/1; Maurice Nimmo: 13/5, 87/3; Pforr: 29/1, 5, 31/1, 3, 57/2, 4, 69/2, 115/3, 173/5, 191/1, 199/4, 223/2; Pott: 27/3, 39/1, 71/1, 75/3, 97/5, 137/1, 163/3, 175/5, 237/2; Reinhard: 2, 3, 9/1, 2, 11/2, 13/1, 2, 15/1, 4, 25/2, 31/2, 5, 35/1, 37/3, 53/1, 63/1, 67/2, 71/2, 73/2, 4, 77/2, 3, 4, 5, 89/2, 93/1, 2, 101/2, 3, 103/1, 105/3, 111/1, 113/1, 3, 115/1, 2, 5, 127/1, 131/1, 133/1, 2, 3, 4, 139/4, 147/1, 151/1, 2, 155/4, 5, 159/1, 2, 165/1, 173/2, 3, 4, 5, 195/1, 207/3, 209/2, 213/1, 2, 213/1, 2, 223/5, 225/1, 2, 229/3, 235/1, 2, 244; Reigisl: 109/1; Reuter: 7/2, 65/3, 83/2, 159/2, 189/3, 219/2; Ian C. Rose: 17/2, 19/5, 25/3 45/3, 47/1, 53/4, 59/1, 81/1, 147/3, 169/3, 229/2; Rosmarion: 19/3, 51/3, 63/4, 65/2, 75/2, 87/2, 89/1, 107/1, 117/4, 123/3, 129/2, 139/3, 149/3, 153/3, 185/1, 2, 189/1, 210/3, U4 (3); Ruckstuhl: 119/4, 167/2, 213/3, 4; Sammer: 43/1, 79/2, 203/1; Siedel: 29/4, 135/3, 205/2; Silvestris:105/4 (Partsch), 107/3 (Schweinsberg), Silvestris Fotoservice: 141/1, 209/3 (Buhler); Singer: 21/1, 85/2, 121/3, 167/3, 219/5, 223/4; Skibbe: 23/2; Scherz: U1 (7), Buchrücken, U4 (4); Skimmitat: 15/2, 41/1, 3, 43/2, 45/4, 47/2, 3, 49/2, 61/1, 69/1, 73/1, 81/3, 4, 87/1, 95/3, 97/1, 119/1, 2, 3, 127/3, 131/3, 135/2, 139/1, 149/2, 5, 155/1, 157/1, 163/1, 2, 169/2, 175/2, 3, 183/2, 185/3, 4, 201/2, 3, 205/1, 207/4, 211/1, 2, 3, 217/3, 221/3, 4, 5, 223/1, 3, 227/2, 233/4; Schmelzenbach: 27/1, 45/2, 125/2, 127/2, 137/5, 139/2, 147/2, 155/3, 181/3, 215/3, 219/3; Schremmer: 73/3; Schrempp: 9/4, 29/2, 39/2, 51/2, 67/3, 91, 1, 3, 133/5, 161/1, 2, 173/1, 175/4, 177/2, 179/3, 215/1, 233/2, 237/1; Stein: 49/4; Vetter: 157/3, 195/2; Maurice Walker: 7/1; Martin Walters: 13/4, 41/4, 55/2, 61/3, 115/4, 141/2, 165/2, 209/1; Tony Wharton: 217/1; O. Willner: 7/3, 191/2, 193/2, 4; W. Willner: 117/2, 209/4, 231/1; Rodger Wilmshurst: 207/5; Wisniewski: 25/4, 129/1, 193/3; Wothe: 19/1, 21/3, 27/2, 33/3, 35/2, 39/3, 41/2, 49/3, 57/5, 59/3, 79/3, 83/1, 87/4, 95/2, 107/4, 117/3, 137/3, 143/3, 145/2, 153/2, 163/4, 5, 179/4, 189/2, 195/3, 207/1, 211/4, 227/1, 3, 233/3; Zettl: 79/1, 103/2